For curious and compassionate rebels
Past, Present and Future

REBEL VEGAN LIFE

A RADICAL NEW TAKE ON VEGANISM
FOR A BRAVE NEW WORLD

TODD SINCLAIR

First published 2021 by Intrepid Fox Publishing Ltd

20-22 Wenlock Road
London N1 7GU

Hardback ISBN 978-1-7398490-2-3
Paperback ISBN 978-1-7398490-1-6
eISBN 978-1-7398490-0-9

RebelVeganLife.com

Original Illustrations by Cathy Brear

Exclusive Thank You Gift
for Rebel Vegan Readers:

FREE Download of Complimentary ebook

TOP 10 VEGAN SUPERFOODS
With Nutritional Guidelines and Recipes

https://rebelveganlife.ck.page/rebelvegansuperfoods

CONTENTS

NOT ANOTHER VEGAN

*"Nothing is more powerful than
an idea whose time has come."*
Victor Hugo

This is not another vegan book

You are not another vegan

REBEL VEGAN LIFE is a three-part message born out of love for the planet, the animals, and ourselves. Together, we will celebrate, demystify, and uncomplicate veganism. This book is about inspiring and empowering everyone to find their sweet spot on the vegan spectrum. Everyone's journey is unique, so within this book are the keys needed to unlock your own plant- based life, feel confident going out into the world as a vegan, and to stick with it in this brave new world.

In the following pages, I will share with you the full history of veganism, as well as an in-depth exposé of our current food system and the urgent issues that have created the modern vegan movement. *REBEL VEGAN* gives you all the wisdom and support needed to live in the world as an informed and confident vegan. We can show you the way, and provide the background inspiration, but it's up to you to choose the way that veganism works best for you.

Before we begin our journey, there's one important thing I need to make clear. This book is a judgment-free zone. Because, let's be honest—the word "vegan" has become a dirty word. A divisive word that is seen by many as an ascetic or extreme lifestyle.

Yet, at its core, veganism is about compassion and justice. There should be nothing extreme or scary about becoming more aware and kind. So, you won't find any guilt-tripping, patronizing, or stereotyping here, and everyone is welcome at this table. I am not the vegan police, and promise not to raid your fridge!

Please feel secure to explore and let your guard down - this is a safe space. If you are open to new ideas, and hearing the truth about a lifestyle shrouded in misinformation, then this is the book for you. After all, how can you make an informed choice without a clear picture of the situation?

The *REBEL VEGAN* philosophy also focuses on rethinking existing rules and preconceptions, taking a fresh look at veganism and, dare I say it, changing the world for the better.

REBEL VEGANS—that's you too, by the way—cherish the role they have to play in creating a kinder world for themselves and others. They seek the truth, know the power of change, and want to make a positive impact. Following an established or orthodox version of veganism is not necessary for this. We are trailblazers after all, not sheep!

> *I predict that future generations will look back at our meat production and consumption with horror and disbelief. fiThis book offers the motivation and means to be on the right side of history.*
> **REBEL VEGAN**

The Vegan Society officially defines the term veganism as: "...a philosophy and way of living which seeks to exclude— as far as is possible and practicable—all forms of exploitation of, and cruelty to, animals for food, clothing or any other purpose; and by extension, promotes the development and use of animal-free alternatives for the benefit of animals, humans and the environment."[1]

With that in mind, *REBEL VEGAN* does not preach one way of living. This isn't a cult, it's a philosophy. You don't blindly apply a set of rules, you interpret and adapt them to suit your unique situation. As you read this book, you can choose the topics that inspire or motivate you on your journey. The definition even allows that veganism goes "as far as is possible and practical." This openness provides lots of room within the vegan space.

The debate can be emotive and polarized. Just look at any vegan group on social media to see the sort of in-fighting that, ironically, goes against the compassion principle of a vegan lifestyle. We should be supporting and motivating each other, not tearing each other down. This is not a one-size-fits-all book. It is about making informed choices, finding alignment in your beliefs, embracing your passions, and enjoying food. I strongly believe that any change you make from a space of compassion will be beneficial, even profound, and help create a better world for everyone.

Wherever you are on the diet spectrum—mindful meat-eater, pescatarian, vegetarian, vegan-curious, or fully plant-based—I celebrate the fact you are here, reading this book and taking steps to lead a kinder and more sustainable life.

Vegans and non-vegans are not on opposite sides. We are in this together, sharing the planet and its resources, and striving to make better choices within our circumstances.

I wasn't always vegan and have experienced both extremes of the diet spectrum. I grew up on a large dairy farm in Canada and spent my adult life traveling the world, learning from different cultures, and trying all the foods they had to offer.

But one day I got ill after eating some dodgy meat from a trusted street vendor in my usual corner of Bangkok.

That put an instant stop to my globe-trotting. I sought refuge with my monk friends in a Buddhist monastery in the cool hills of Vietnam. There, my old friends nurtured me back to health on a lacto-vegetarian diet. For someone who had always considered dairy and meat to be a key part of a healthy, balanced diet, it was a revelation.

I didn't convert to Buddhism, but I did become a vegan.

I have been vegan for five years now, and I have never felt healthier, happier, or more aligned with my choices and impact on the world. There is a sense of contentment and confidence in choosing foods that are right for both my body and the planet. This book was born out of my own struggles and triumphs as I transitioned to a fully plant-based lifestyle. REBEL VEGAN is a love letter to the new vegan in all of us. I hope it challenges and inspires you in equal measures to build your best life.

This is a critical time to consider a lifestyle change as we build a new normal in a changing world. As we stumble out of lockdowns and the world opens up again, many of us are searching for new ways to live our lives. We no longer view the world and how it works as locked in or unchangeable. It's time to reimagine and create new systems and lifestyles that puts our health, ethics, and sustainability at the forefront. We can be the change we want to see.

Use this book as your guide to understanding these connected but complex issues, and to empower you to make the shift from pre-Covid to an improved and new normal. Covid was a once-in-a-lifetime opportunity to pause and reset, even to reinvent our lives.

We've known for years that the way we produce certain foods harms our planet. And now, thanks to articles in the British Medical Journal, we know that the food industry is at least partly responsible for the severity of Covid-19[2]. How we live, how we eat, and how we relate to our environment matters now more than ever. Veganism is the most positive and powerful step we can take. This means making decisions based on a love for the planet, the animals, and ourselves as human beings.

I think we can all agree that the world is changing and we will have to change with it. The information in the following chapters will support you to come out as vegan, in whatever way that works best for you.

**So welcome to the table, fellow rebels.
Let's veganize our lives.**

1

RECLAIMING OUR HISTORY

"Knowledge is power.
And power should always
be used with compassion."
REBEL VEGAN

There is a common misconception that veganism is a modern-day fad that will have its moment and fizzle out in due course like other trendy diets. So it was important for me to search through history to find our brave ancestors and reclaim our overlooked but proud past. It was like tracing our family tree. Their rebellious voices and activism came echoing back through the centuries and gave me strength.

I think history is essential to understanding and appreciating who we are. It can give us power and a sense of purpose. That's what is so beautiful when you realize you connect to others who came before you. They become our forefathers/mothers and a divine source of power that you can draw on whenever you need that boost.

First and foremost, the rejoinder to the fad-diet myth is a resounding NO. Veganism is far from a fad. The latest research[1] into our early ancestors shows we weren't the meat-eating predators depicted by conventional history books or the Flintstones. Another clue lies in religious scriptures, which advocate against violence of all kinds, including violence towards animals. Even ancient Greek philosophy is full of arguments against eating animals.

With that said, the answer is also yes. The vegan diet is trending. There is no denying that veganism has enjoyed a resurgence in present times as a response to the growing and frightening crisis we face today. As we open our minds to explore plant-based living, it is useful, and indeed powerful, to stand back and get some perspective on what is an age-old philosophy. Modern veganism is a type of rebalancing. It offers an answer to our world's current challenges.

The start of the vegan movement is often dated to the invention of the word "vegan" in 1944.

Although that's when Western society first acknowledged it as a lifestyle option, ethical eating has its roots in both prehistory and ancient history.

THE MYTH OF THE HUNTER-GATHERER

It was famed anthropologist Raymond Dart who, after discovering the first fossil of one of our ancestors in Africa, planted the notion of the meat-eating prehistoric man. He described our ancestors as: *"...carnivorous creatures that seized living quarries by violence, battered them to death, slaking their ravenous thirst with the hot blood of victims and greedily devouring livid writhing flesh.[2]"*

Talk about making early humans sound barbaric!

We have been fed an alpha-male fairytale of brave, muscled cavemen thrusting spears and killing large game for food. The emphasis has been firmly on the "hunter" element of our ancestors. It is time to revisit this, bring in some modern findings, and reclaim our history.

Do you remember the Flintstones? They have a lot to answer for. We imagine cavemen hunting mammoths and saber-tooth tigers, but there is little evidence that this happened on any scale. Don't trust those upper-Paleolithic cave paintings. You might have been told that these depict traditional hunting scenes, but you should know that it is thought our cavemen ancestors were overly creative and had an inflated ego. An increasingly accepted theory is that cave paintings are depictions of visions and hallucinations, rather than actual events. This hypothesis has been advanced several times in the last decade, most recently by the Journal of Archeology, Consciousness and Culture.[3]

Given that humans cannot tear flesh or hide by hand, it is very likely that our earliest ancestors only turned to animal flesh out of necessity, when their usual staples were unavailable. They were opportunistic hunters of meat, only taking the easy kill.[4]

These ancestors began fashioning crude stone tools around 2.5 million years ago.[5] They had two main priorities: survival and reproduction. Their primary focus on a daily basis was gathering food. Working in small groups, they would go into the woods, rivers, and grasslands to see what could be found to eat that day.

When the tools and rudimentary weapons entered the scene, did we turn into big-time hunters? Early humans caught bugs, tree squirrels, fish, rabbits, and other small wild animals.[6] But the vast majority of their diet consisted of native, wild plants, such as roots, fruits, nuts, seeds, and vegetables. We were not exclusively herbivores, but we definitely weren't exclusively carnivores either. Our diet was similar to our closest relatives—the other large primates. Seeing as we share over 96% of our DNA with chimpanzees,[7] it's no great leap of faith to assume we probably shared the same diet back in the day.[8] The primate diet is an omnivorous diet. They eat plants (fruits, flowers, leaves, nuts, seeds, and grasses) supplemented by small animals (birds, birds' eggs, lizards, small rodents, frogs, and insects).

Alternatively, let's put it another way: do we look like carnivores to you?

Would you have survived in the wild? This is a question that the Greek philosopher Plutarch wrote about in his essays on eating meat. Look at the structure of our bodies. Do we have hooked beaks, sharp talons, or jagged teeth? Do we even have enough stomach acid to break down a diet made up mostly of flesh?

2,000 years ago, Plutarch argued what modern science has since explained, that the softness of our body, our small mouth, flat teeth, and our digestive system are not designed by nature to hunt. If we were carnivorous animals, we would hunt like tigers or lions. We would use our fangs and our claws to tear down a gazelle, a boar, or a lamb. We would eat it while it was still alive, the way predatory animals do.

Oh, wait, we don't have fangs. And as for eating our prey as the life flutters out of them, Plutarch asks: *"If you have qualms about eating the flesh while life is still present, why do you continue, contrary to nature, to eat what possesses life?*[9]*"*

It is a powerful question, worth pondering. Our meat must be dead, sanitized, boiled, roasted, fried, and seasoned with spices or herbs (plants!) to make it palatable. Or, as Plutarch puts it, in order that: *"... the palate may be deceived and accept what is foreign to it."*

Even if we go down the road of the sophisticated carnivore—making up for what we lacked in physical ability with weapons—the picture of a meat-centric diet still doesn't add up. Hunting is hard work. It is dangerous. The dedicated Hada and Kung bushmen of Africa, who hunt with bows and arrows, fail to get any meat more than half the time. Wild animals aren't just hanging around waiting to be caught.

The truth is hunter-gatherers did not eat meat that often. According to research published in National Geographic[10], hunter-gatherers received approximately 30% of their annual calories from meat, and this wasn't even a consistent measure. In fact, they endured lean times when meat was limited to less than a handful of meat a week. There is no denying that our early ancestor's activities included some hunting, but it was not the method by which they obtained most of their food.

So, what was?

Well, it turns out that "man the hunter" was backed up by "woman the forager." According to anthropologists, almost 70% of the hunter-gatherer diet was made up of plants including tubers, nuts, roots, fruits, and grains. The story that hunting and meat-eating made us human is flawed. The truth is our ancestors might have turned to meat at times, but they survived on a predominantly plant-based diet.[11]

Based on this, you could say that a plant-based diet is far from a fad—it is actually millions of years old. In fact, we vegans have a rich past. Our diet has been a cause for debates that have echoed through the centuries. Veganism is as old as recorded history, and it has kept us alive and enlightened throughout the ages.

RELIGION AND VEGAN VALUES

"Around the time that homo-sapiens were elevated as divine status by humanist religions, farm animals stopped being viewed as living creatures who could feel pain and distress, and instead came to be treated as machines. They spend their entire lives as cogs in a production line, and the quality and length of their lives is determined by the profit and losses of business corporations."
Yuval Noah Harari on animal agriculture[12]

Our early ancestors had a spiritual relationship with their fellow animals. Cave paintings and ancient art give us a clue that animals were closely linked with divinity. So it is hardly surprising that the earliest people to adopt what is now known as a vegetarian or vegan diet were religious and spiritual followers.

The world's most practiced religions have all advocated against cruelty towards animals. They each have their own teachings and scriptures surrounding animals and their place in the world. Animals have traditionally played a role in religious ceremonies, meals, and even sacrifices. Some religions consider animals sacred, while others consider them a source of food, but for the most part, they have a deep respect for all that God created, including animals and plants. However, just like the concepts of love, forgiveness, and unity can be turned around to encourage wars (like the Christian crusades of the Middle Ages), religion has sometimes been used as justification for harming animals. We are witnessing the result of this disregard for life in the environmental and animal welfare crisis we are currently facing. Let's take a closer look at what the world's principal religions say about animals.

JUDAISM - ORIGINATED IN 2085 BC
Judaism believes animals are part of God's creation. It therefore calls for the proper treatment of animals and asks humans to avoid causing pain to any living creatures. One of the Jewish codes of law mandates that animals should be treated with compassion, and that a Jew cannot pass by an animal in distress or animals being mistreated, even on the Sabbath.

HINDUISM - ORIGINATED IN 1500 BC

Hinduism believes all creatures have a soul, and that they are part of the supreme soul—the god-like energy that brings all things into being. I have been to temples in Indonesia with animal gods like Nandi the bull. Some animals are sacrificed in Hindu ceremonies, but the animal must be treated with great care leading up to the event. Treating animals with kindness and respect is part of a Hindu's way of life.

BUDDHISM - ORIGINATED IN 560 BC

Buddhism is based on the Vedic Scriptures written in 1200 BC. These scriptures promote the concept of ahimsa, or "non-violence." Ahimsa is the virtue of inflicting no harm to any living being, so that your spirit stays pure. Many teachings clearly advocate staying away from eating meat. So as not to become a source of violence, followers of Buddhism were encouraged to establish kindness by not eating meat. To them, meat is for wild beasts; it is unfitting to eat it.[13]

Five ethical teachings govern how Buddhists live. One of these teachings prohibits taking the life of any person or animal. Followers of Buddhism usually follow a lacto-vegetarian diet. This means they consume dairy products, but exclude eggs, poultry, fish, and meat from their diet.

The Buddha himself is known to believe that eating meat destroys great compassion, and advises his disciples to avoid the consumption of meat, just as they would avoid the flesh of their own children.

CHRISTIANITY - ORIGINATED IN 30 AD

Christian teachings state that everything in the universe owes its existence to God, and therefore this provides a basis for opting for a vegan diet. Many leading notable Christians treated animals with high regards and compassion. For example, St Francis of Assisi is known to have preached to the birds, while St Antony of Padua preached to fish.[14] Genesis 1 states God created all creatures and made them good. Psalm 145 states God has compassion and provides for every living thing. Luke 12.6 mentions that not a single sparrow is forgotten in God's sight.

The book of Genesis states: *"God said, 'See, I have given you every plant yielding seed that is upon the face of all the earth, and every tree with seed in its fruit; you shall have them for food. And to every beast of the earth, and to every bird of the air, and to everything that creeps on the earth, everything that has the breath of life, I have given every green plant for food.' And so it was."* [15]

The accepted interpretation of these verses is that God created the world vegan. But it goes further. The Bible also speaks of God's intentions, his idea of a "peaceable kingdom" is one where: *"The wolf shall live with the lamb, the leopard shall lie down with the kid, the calf and the lion and the falling together, and a little child shall lead them. The cow and the bear shall graze, their young shall lie down together; and the lion shall eat straw like the ox."* [16]

The Bible tells of a world where no animals are killed for food. While many Christians believe that all God's creatures can feel pain and suffering, and should therefore be treated with kindness, others view this from a different standpoint—the standpoint of human dominion. Christian texts have been interpreted so wildly that even meat eaters can justify their dietary choices. This justification comes in the form of downgrading animals by suggesting that God created animals solely for the use of humans, and that animals were inferior because they had no soul. However, Jesus himself made comments that implies animals are endowed with a soul and to be cherished. When he was sending his disciples out into the world to spread the gospel, he told the disciples to preach to them. Mark 16:15 *"And he said unto them, Go ye into all the world, and preach the gospel to every creature.*[17]*"* It is clear that at the root of Christianity is love for everything that God has created. Is there any better way to show love and respect to these creations than by following Jesus' lead?

ISLAM - ORIGINATED IN 610 AD
Islamic religion calls for using animals when necessary, but cruelty towards an animal is considered a sin. In his teachings, prophet Muhammad states that mercy towards animals will be rewarded, and that both animals and humans should be treated with kindness.

All these religions, rooted as they are in respect for what God or a higher power has created, may not specifically advocate a vegan diet, but do ask their followers to be mindful of how they treat other sentient beings. Today we would call that a cruelty-free lifestyle. In other words, living a life of kindness.

Perhaps religious teachings fall short of advocating complete abstinence from meat, because they were written at a time when using animals for food did not have the environmental and social implications it has today, and when we lacked the structural, technological, and pharmaceutical knowledge to create the extreme industrial farms. Regardless, they tell their followers that cruelty towards animals is wrong. They all agree that when an animal must be killed or be of service for transport, it should be treated with respect and kindness. For example, the Torah states:

> *"Since the desire of procuring food necessitates the slaying of animals, the Torah commands that the death of the animal should be the easiest. It is not allowed to torment the animal by cutting the throat in a clumsy manner, by piercing it, or by cutting off a limb while the animal is still alive."* [18]

Before we developed monotheism, the pagan world celebrated and cherished animals. Multi-god religions tend to connect humans and their environment. There are gods of nature, gods of wine, and gods of animals. Some gods were part animal, such as the Egyptian goddess Isis (often depicted as a cow, or with the horns of a cow[19]), or the Greek god Chiron (half man, half horse[20]). Instead, over the years, monotheistic religions appear to have elevated man above his environment and other living things, leading to the crisis we face today. Animals have become commodities, here for the sole purpose of being used by man. As such, we turn away as the worst atrocities are committed against them.

Something appears to have gone wrong. Somewhere along the way, we have forgotten these teachings. We have lost our way.

GREEK PHILOSOPHY AND VEGANISM

Ancient Greece, which we most often associate with wine-fueled orgies and a plethora of horny gods, was actually the venue for an ancient debate on the topic of justice for animals. Early veganism was actually referred to as *"abstinence from beings with a soul[21]."*

One of the first Greek philosophers to promote a vegan lifestyle was Pythagoras. Born in 569 BC, he is best known for being a classical superstar and the founding father of mathematics, music, astronomy, and philosophy. His teachings influenced Plato and Aristotle, and he was an early champion of women's education.

As if that wasn't enough, he was the first philosopher on record to promote an ethical diet. He believed that all creatures are created equal and should therefore be treated with respect. He also believed that eating meat caused people to become more violent towards each other.[22]

Due to his teachings, the first self-proclaimed vegetarians called themselves "Pythagoreans." These original *REBEL VEGANS* were not about self-denial or vague spiritual concepts. Following in his footsteps, they advanced a grounded theory on the treatment of animals. They believed that any being that experiences pain or suffering should not have pain inflicted on it unnecessarily. Because to Pythagoras, vegetarianism, pacifism, and humane treatment of other sentient beings are all part of a path towards inner peace and world peace.[23]

Five hundred years later, another respected philosopher and Delphi priest, Plutarch (who was inspired by Pythagorean philosophy), went on record to defend the animals and debunk some of the arguments that are still being used today, 2000 years later, in defense of meat-eating. It's a case of history repeating itself.

And there are more. Apollonius of Tayna, as a Pythagorean, opposed animal sacrifice and lived on a frugal, strictly vegetarian diet.[24] Plotinus, a Greek philosopher who avoided any products or medicines made from animals, considered interconnectedness and ethics inseparable. He said: *"If my soul and your soul come from the soul of the All and that soul is one, these souls must also be one, allowing us to feel one another's feelings."* [25]

We have come so far in modern times, with our technology and our conquest of space, and yet in some ways we have stood still or even regressed. When it comes to our humaneness and compassion for other animals, we still have much work to do. You, as a *REBEL VEGAN*, are helping put kindness back on the map.

"All beings tremble before death. All fear death.
When you consider this, you will not kill or cause someone
to kill. All beings fear before danger. Life is dear to all."
Dhammapada - Buddhist Scripture

THE FIRST ANIMAL RIGHTS ACTIVIST?

PLUTARCH'S ESSAYS ON VEGANISM 66 AD:[26]

"For the sake of a little flesh we deprive them of the sun, of the light, of the duration of life to which they are entitled by birth and being.

We declare, then, that it is absurd for them to say that the practice of flesh-eating is based on nature. For that man is not naturally carnivorous is, in the first place, obvious from the structure of his body. A man's frame is in no way similar to those creatures who were made for flesh-eating; he has no hooked beak or sharp nails or jagged teeth, no strong stomach or warmth of vital fluids able to digest and assimilate a heavy diet of flesh. It is from the very fact, the evenness of our teeth, the smallness of our mouths, the softness of our tongues, our possession of vital fluids too inert to digest meat that nature disavows our eating of flesh.

If you declare that you are naturally designed for such a diet, then first kill for yourself what you want to eat. Do it however, only through your own resources, unaided by cleaver or cudgel of any kind or axe. Rather, just as wolves and bears and lions themselves slay what they eat, so you are to fell an ox with your fangs or a boar with your jaws, or tear a lamb or hare in bits. Fall upon it and eat it still living, as animals do. But if you wait for what you eat to be dead, if you have qualms about enjoying the flesh while life is still present, why do you continue, contrary to nature, to eat what possesses life?

Even when it is lifeless and dead, however, no one eats the flesh just as it is; men boil it and roast it, altering it by fire and drugs, recasting and diverting and smothering with countless condiments the taste of gore so that the palate may be deceived and accept what is foreign to it."

We should learn from our forefather, The First *REBEL VEGAN*.

VEGAN LEADERS AND RULERS

Egyptian Pharaoh Akhenaten (1353-1336 BC): *banned animal sacrifice because he believed it was a sin to take away any given life by the god Aten. Interestingly, Akhenaten has been described as revolutionary and as "the greatest idealist in the world." No doubt this is at least partly due to his approach to animal rights.*[27]

Japanese Emperor Tenmu (673-686 AD): *banned the consumption of domesticated animal meat (horses, cattle, dogs, monkeys and birds) between April 1st and September 30th of each year as a nod to Buddhist teachings.*[28]

"Animals should not be consumed but should be viewed as prized gifts from God. That is the way of a whole human being."
Abraham Lincoln[29]

"Eating flesh is unproved murder."
Benjamin Franklin[30]

"The life of a lamb is no less precious than that of a human being. The more helpless the creature, the more that it is entitled to protection by man from the cruelty of man."
Mohandas Gandhi

RENAISSANCE AND ENLIGHTENMENT

During the Renaissance period between the 14th and 17th century, vegetarian ideology was rare. Meat was a scarce luxury, available only for the rich. At this time, Greek philosophies from thinkers like Pythagoras were rediscovered and became influential again. The notion that animals feel pain and therefore deserve consideration was again being debated. Luigi Cornaro, a Venetian nobleman and dietitian who lived to 99 years of age, spoke out about the excesses of the elite classes and adopted a vegetarian diet. Desiderius Eramus, a Dutch humanist, Thomas More, a social philosopher, and Michel de Montaigne, one of the best known philosophers of the French Renaissance, were appalled by the brutal practices associated with blood sports, writing with passion about the plight of animals. Leonardo Da Vinci is also on record as denouncing meat-eating.

The Enlightenment period in the 18th century marked a new view of man's place in the order of creation—above all animals. The philosopher René Descartes advanced the notion that animals do not have souls, and introduced the concept of animals as machines. However, not all were in alignment with this. John Locke, British philosopher, argued that animals are, in fact, intelligent. Among western religions, there was a re-emergence of the idea that eating animals was an aberration of God's will and human nature. Other famous vegetarians of this period include poets Alexander Pope and John Gay, the royal physician, Dr. John Arbuthnot, and the creator of the Methodist movement, John Wesley[31]. Dr. George Cheyne was a pioneering physician of his time, well-known for going vegetarian to recover from obesity-related health problems. He was an early advocate of the lacto-vegetarian diet. Although the medical community criticized it at the time, his book *An Essay of Health and Long Life* was a huge success.[32] Around this time, British philosopher Jeremy Bentham is known for comparing animal suffering to that of humans.

"The question is not 'can they reason?'
Nor 'can they talk?' But 'can they suffer?'"
Jeremy Bentham[33], 1789

The 19th century saw many radical thinkers promoting vegetarianism. Dr. William Lambe, for example, was a prominent figure in both the medical and literary worlds, and would influence Dr. John Newton, who later set up The Vegetarian Society. The romantic poet Percy Shelley was convinced of the health benefits of a meat-free diet, and was vegetarian. He also went political with his diet choices, pointing out that inefficient use of resources meant that meat production was one of the reasons for food shortages among the neediest people[34].

A BRAVE NEW VEGAN WORLD

"We can see quite plainly that our present civilisation is built on the exploitation of animals, just as past civilisations were built on the exploitation of slaves, and we believe the spiritual destiny of man is such that in time he will view with abhorrence the idea that men once fed on the products of animals' bodies."
Donald Watson, in the first issue of The Vegan News 1944[35].

The year 1809 marks the start of a movement towards vegetarianism as an expression of Christian faith, when Reverend William Cowherd established the Bible Christian Church and began using biblical references to appeal against meat-eating. This church, together with members of a reforming educational college, Alcott House and the Northwood Villa Infirmary, formed the Vegetarian Society in 1847. Three years later, William Metcalfe, a member of the Bible Christian Church, emigrated to the US with members of his congregation and set up the American Vegetarian Society.[36]

In the 1830s, the concept of vegetarianism was born. At this time, technological leaps meant agriculture was becoming more intensive, and the rise of larger scale animal farming was beginning to raise questions about the ethics of eating animals. Early vegetarianism included clothing and other aspects of life, and was therefore comparable to veganism. However, when the Vegetarian Society was established, a vegetarian diet included eggs and dairy. In 1849, the first ever vegan book was published. It was a cookery book that excluded butter and eggs. Having said that, the concept and term "vegan" had yet to be invented.

At the dawn of the new 20th century, between 1909 and 1912, members of the Vegetarian Society had lively discussions about whether vegetarians should eat eggs and dairy products. In 1923, the editor of the Vegetarian Messenger wrote: *"We feel that the ideal position for vegetarians is abstinence from animal products and that most of us are, like other reformers, in a transitional stage."*[37]

Then, as the Vegetarian Society was at war, the editor wrote in 1935: *"The question as to whether dairy products should be used by vegetarians becomes more pressing year by year."*[38]

The schism opened up further when the secretary of the Leicester branch, Donald Watson, challenged this position and their indecision. At the time, Donald had been a vegetarian for seven years, after witnessing the brutal slaughter of pigs on his uncle's farm, but now he had begun to question the ethics of dairy. Having experimented with a diet free from all animal products and found it "varied, appetizing, and in every way satisfactory," he and Elsie Shrigley, a fellow activist, suggested that a subgroup of non-dairy vegetarians be formed within the Vegetarian Society.[39] When their request was refused, they decided to set up a new society and quarterly magazine.

And so, on a sunny Sunday afternoon in 1944, Donald Watson, Elsie Shrigley, and four other rebels met in the Attic Club in London to discuss the birth of a groundbreaking organization. And the first thing on the agenda was to settle on a name for this brave new movement. Among the options were "dairyban," "vitan" and "benevore." I don't know about you, but I'm glad they settled for vegan, which was the winning pick as it contained the first three and the last two letters of "vegetarian." Donald Watson said it marked "the beginning and the end of vegetarian." A typically bold statement from our founder, especially when you consider the first Vegan Society newsletter went out to just twenty-five subscribers.[40]

However, the initial response was promising and attracted more than 100 supporters, including a celebrity endorsement from playwright George Bernard Shaw[41] who pledged to abandon eggs and dairy. This rebel movement had begun in earnest and would only gather momentum in response to the escalating atrocities of industrial farming in the last half of the 20th century.

It wasn't until 1949 that the official definition of veganism was established: "A philosophy and way of living which seeks to exclude—as far as is possible and practicable—all forms of exploitation of, and cruelty to, animals for food, clothing or any other purpose; and by extension, promotes the development and use of animal-free alternatives for the benefit of humans, animals and the environment. In dietary terms, it denotes the practice of dispensing with all products derived wholly or partly from animals."[42]

Although veganism remained very much a little-known niche movement throughout much of the 20th century, the counterculture movements of the Sixties and Seventies increased its popularity. More and more young people were traveling to places like India and discovering spirituality, yoga, mindfulness, and peaceful lifestyle options.

What's more, the Sixties also marked the rise of fast-food outlets and the rapid growth of infrastructure and technologies needed to supply an increasing demand for cheap meat. These brutal advances helped focus the rebels in the underground vegan movement to find their voices and advance the urgency and necessity of veganism.

Fast-forward to the time of writing, 2021, and veganism is on the up, in a big way. But it isn't a victory... yet. Never before have we consumed as much meat, dairy, and eggs as we do today. Even so, the vegan movement has exploded in the last decade. In the US, the number of vegans rose from 4 million to 20 million between 2014 and 2018, a 600% increase. In the UK, the number of people identifying as vegan has quadrupled since 2014, going from 150,000 to 720,000.[43]

Despite this unprecedented growth, veganism would have to grow at the same rate for 30 years before the whole world became vegan. Globally, it's estimated that there are around 79 million vegans— that's just 1% of the world's population.

The Economist termed 2019 *"The Year of The Vegan."* What has happened in recent times to spur this on? Why has there been a sudden surge in veganism in the 21st century?

There is no straight-forward answer, but I think it is part of a domino effect caused by many factors all coming together at once. A huge component of this is the internet, and the fact we have access to information like never before—we have encyclopedias at our fingertips. Millennials and Generation Z's have run with this. Social media has been a tool to spread the message far and wide, creating digital communities of *REBEL VEGANS* who all share the same passion. Of course, it has its dangers and pitfalls, but one can't deny it has been key to inspiring us all to rethink our eating habits.

I am hopeful it might just save the world. In a way, social media has replaced direct action as the way to bring about social change.

Organizations like *Anonymous for the Voiceless* would not be half as active without social media and the internet to share their message and show what happens behind the locked doors and barbed wires of slaughterhouses. However, it is important that these movements get offline too. Spreading awareness online is only the first step.

It seems we are just starting to wake up—this is only the beginning. It's been a long process. In 2005, *Earthlings* aired for the first time, narrated by Joaquin Phoenix—an almost-too-hard-to-watch documentary shining a light on humankind's dependence on animals for economic purposes, and the exploitation happening across five areas: food, entertainment, medicine, clothing and the pet industry. In 2011, the film *Forks Over Knives* gave us a sobering look at the effect of meat and dairy on our health, linking it to the obesity and heart disease crises.

Cowspiracy hit our screens in 2014, with its focus on the environmental impact of animal agriculture and statistics that had many who watched it committing to at least reducing their meat consumption. Veganism was becoming sexy. Hollywood stars were funding documentaries about it. Celebrities were coming out and sharing their vegan diets.

Veganism stopped being something extreme or annoying and started looking like a desirable lifestyle—the colorful breakfast Buddha bowls probably helped.

Simultaneously, the climate crisis has been getting more and more airtime. It has been at the center of global conversation for most of the 21st century. Unfortunately, there has been little political drive for real change. The internet exposed these political flaws and inspired people—particularly young people— to take matters into their own hands. This is hardly surprising, as they will face the consequences of previous generations' blasé attitude to ecology. Greta Thunberg is perhaps the best example of a young activist with the knowledge and passion to inspire others to join the cause.[44]

Although decreasing carbon emissions and fossil fuels are at the center of this issue, the vegan movement stands firmly alongside this, given that agriculture is responsible for a significant part of high carbon emissions and loss of biodiversity. We are an integral part of the solution. No climate survival remedy is possible without a huge shift in the way we eat. This is something we'll explore further in the Driving Forces chapters.

With all this information at our fingertips, many have become increasingly outraged and frightened at the effects of our diets. But you know what? We have not seen anything yet. The climate crisis, as mind-numbingly frightening as it is, remains pretty abstract, especially for many of us in the Western world. Warmer summers almost sound like a pleasant side effect of unrestrained consumerism. As for the health crisis, it's easy to imagine that this is just something that happens to people with no self-control. Covid however, forces us to really look at how we live, how we eat, and how this impacts both the world and us as individuals.

Could this global health disaster actually help us rebalance the way we live?

Are we humble enough to learn these lessons and driven enough to make changes? I sincerely hope so.

We still have a chance to turn the tide. The resurgence of veganism in the last few years is a direct response to the more pressing crises we face, crises that we will cover in more detail in the next few chapters. And now Covid has come along and shone a light on a problem that scientists have been talking about for years, but that hasn't really hit the headlines: antibiotic-resistant viruses, how meat damages our immune systems, and how it opens the door to further epidemics like the one the world is only recovering from.

So, back to where we started: Is veganism a modern-day fad?

The answer is no.

Our earliest ancestors evolved on a mainly plant-based diet, both from necessity and limited hunting ability. Ethical eating and compassion for animals have been part of our earliest religions and philosophies—respecting other beings was considered a way of respecting God. For the last seven decades, veganism has become a well-defined and strong movement, spurred on not only by animal welfare, but also due to the fact that our current meat-centric diets threaten our very existence.

This is what we are fighting for. As part of the vegan movement, you are a rebel joining the fight for justice and compassion.

FIVE REASONS WHY HUMANS AREN'T DESIGNED TO EAT MEAT:

1. We don't like blood. 99.9% of humans cannot stand the sight of blood and intestines, nor the sounds of an animal dying. Most of us can't stomach the bloody reality of eating an animal.

2. We lack the physical tools. Real carnivores have large canine teeth and sharp claws that can tear flesh from prey. Humans have small, dull canines and short soft fingernails. Humans also have flat molars like herbivores, to grind plant foods like fruit and vegetables.

3. Our digestive systems can't take it. Carnivores have short digestive tracts that allow meat to pass quickly through their system. The human digestive tract is much longer, which gives the fiber and nutrients in plant foods enough time to be broken down and absorbed.

4. We don't have the right stomach acid. Carnivores have strong stomach acid that can break down raw meat and kill any bacteria present. Human stomach acid is similar to plant-eating animals. It is strong, but not strong enough to kill some bacteria found in meat. This is why we must cook meat to eat it. But cooking meat at high temperatures creates substances (heterocyclic amines and polycyclic aromatic hydrocarbons) that cause DNA mutations and increase the risk of cancer.

5. Meat makes us sick. According to the American Heart Association, meat eaters have a 32% higher risk of developing heart disease than vegetarians[45]. If we are meant to eat meat, then why does it make us sick?

2

MEAT CORRUPTION

"The world will not be destroyed by those who do evil, but by those who watch them without doing anything."
Albert Einstein[1]

We have touched on how the vegan movement has grown and is building momentum, but why has it become so urgent and essential at this moment?

Before we dive deeper into the motivational driving forces, let's take a look at our current food system and the mess in which we find ourselves. To find our way out, we have to understand why we find ourselves at this point in history.

There are forces at play keeping us stuck in a situation that threatens our survival. Where once we could only kill a handful of animals with our rudimentary spears, the meat industry has, over the last 250 years, grown into a monster that threatens to kill us all.

We need to wade through the murky waters of the current food system to understand why the meat industry has grown into a beast that threatens our survival. Much of it has to do with what happened after the Second World War. Industrialization, government subsidies, and even the scientific community created the perfect storm and the necessary conditions for this sector to expand to such a degree that it is now one of the most powerful industries in the history of the world: a sector worth an annual two trillion dollars[2] and producing 340 million tons of meat per year.[3]

Another reason this industry has grown exponentially is that it keeps us coming back for more, with a little help from governments, health institutions, and clever marketing.

How could the vegan movement not respond to this? After all, every force has its opposite. As the meat industry grows, so does the counterforce, a movement dedicated to protecting animals and the planet from the effects of our human "progress." Being a *REBEL VEGAN* has never been so urgent—we need rebellious spirits more than ever.

I like to keep faith that since we created this mess, we can clean it up. But time is running out. We are facing many tipping points, and veganism has never been so essential.

We can see this clearly with the industrial and agricultural revolutions. Both are celebrated as wonderful events without which we would all still be living in mud-huts, scratching a meager sustenance from barren fields. While it isn't all bad (I recognize the blessings and advantages of our globalized world—my local corner store has exotic fruits and vegetables from around the globe, and I am grateful for that), these revolutions have come at a high price. I'm no longer sure we got a good deal in the bargain.

FROM FORAGERS TO FARMERS

The first agricultural revolution that changed our world forever is thought to have begun around 12,000 years ago. Foragers became farmers, going from a nomadic hunter-gatherer lifestyle to a more settled way of life that included growing cereal and domesticating animals. This shift from nomadic to settled continued and spread across the globe. Domesticated animals did not just provide an additional source of food, they also made large scale farming possible (a bull pulling a plow goes much faster than a man on his own). This created increasingly stable populations and a move towards the type of settlements we know today: towns and cities.[4]

The agricultural revolution is often viewed as the time when our wild nomadic ancestors finally began to become "civilized." But there are question marks over whether this was all that positive. The latest retelling of our human history, *Sapiens* by Yuval Noah Harari, offers a different perspective. Yes, farms meant more food was available, but this additional food didn't necessarily mean a better diet nor a better life. Farmers were at the mercy of their crops and had a less varied diet than their nomadic foraging counterparts. This agricultural revolution also triggered the appearance of a completely new life-form on earth—the domesticated animal. As the centuries passed, the tables turned and this life-form became the new norm. Today, 90% of all large animals are domesticated.

Far from being an unprecedented improvement, the agricultural revolution created new kinds of suffering which have grown steadily worse with each passing century. Animals are the biggest victims of history. We have captured them, mutilated them, enslaved them, and continue to kill them. Except we no longer do it out of necessity, like a lion kills a gazelle.

We do it for profit.

FROM FARMERS TO FRANKENSTEINERS

The first agricultural revolution of 12,000 BC paved the way for the industrial revolution that began in 1840. This saw us leaving behind traditional methods, such as crop rotation that restored and maintained soil quality, to adopting the modern practices we have today. In the mid-18th century, two British agriculturalists, Thomas Coke and Robert Bakewell, introduced selective breeding and inbreeding to reduce genetic diversity. Bakewell was the first person to breed cattle to be used exclusively for meat.

This was an interesting time. In the Western world, religious teachings were on shaky ground. This was a period of intellectual and religious upheaval. People began to question whether there really was a God, and whether everything on this earth was indeed a divine creation that needed to be respected and cared for. Plato's view of the universe as an intelligent living being[5] was being eroded by a new theory, that of a mechanical universe. It sparked the rise of the modern metropolis, factories and the individual.

This philosophy of an unthinking, mechanical universe where things act according to strict laws of nature creates the perfect backdrop for the industrial revolution and the global economic shifts that followed. At this time, René Descartes also argued that the only creatures to have been endowed with a soul were humans, which left animals stripped of the soul and the ability to feel. Conveniently, this made it acceptable to treat them in whatever way humans deemed necessary or beneficial.

As atheism grew in popularity, even human beings stopped being endowed with a divine soul. We went from being children of a higher power to biological happenings, here purely by accident. Darwin's "survival of the fittest" theory conspired to place humans at the top of an animal hierarchy, from which we could express our dominion over other creatures. Ironically, we have now taken it to such an extreme that we face a situation where our treatment of animals threatens our survival on this planet. This set the scene. The wheels of progress were in motion, and there was no turning back.

In the early 1900s, around half of the population were farmers or lived in rural communities. Farms produced various crops, and different animals were present together and used in complementary ways (for example, keeping horses and using the manure to fertilize soil). Animals typically had access to the outdoors. Most of the work was done by human or animal labor.

In the 1950s, technology and specialization began to take over. Big farms got larger, while small farms closed down. Fields of diverse crops gave way to monocultures of genetically identical crops—particularly corn, wheat, and soy. Milk, egg, and meat production became separate from crop production. These facilities housed a single breed of animal during one period of its lifespan. Selective breeding meant animals were being bred for a single outcome, such as increased milk production, rather than being part of the life of the farm.

Chemical and pharmaceutical advances conspired to make things both more brutally efficient and less humane. Synthetic fertilizers and chemical pesticides were introduced in the early 1900s, became widespread in the 50s, and then enjoyed exponential growth. Today, we use 5.6 billion pounds of pesticides globally every year, with devastating consequences for our health and the environment.[6] Pharmaceuticals also became commonplace in the newly industrialized production of milk, egg, and meat. Experiments in the 1940s and 50s found that antibiotics made animals gain weight faster, and by 2009 80% of the antibiotic drugs sold in the US were used in livestock production.[7]

What drove this push for bigger farms? It wasn't just that new technology enabled these operations. Economics and government were at play. Government policies encouraged farmers to scale up. In the late 1950s, for example, the US secretary of agriculture, Ezra Taft Benson, called on farmers to "Get big or get out." These days, we have a situation where the majority of food production and agriculture is carried out by a small handful of large companies. In the US, 82% of the earnings from cattle slaughter are split between four corporations.[8]

Some will have you believe this is how we get better products and cheaper prices. For the most part, the opposite is true. With fewer competitors, dominant companies have more power to influence prices in their favor. They can also dictate how food is produced and can lobby the government to enact policies that suit them.

It's not about creating better consumer products, but about achieving a higher profit margin at the cost of much suffering.

THE ROLE OF SCIENCE

Alongside this exposition in technical know-how, scientific know-how also grew in leaps and bounds. Unfortunately, progress in the wrong hands can have devastating consequences.

In traditional societies, such as ancient Egypt, the Roman Empire, or medieval Europe, humans had a very limited understanding of zoology, biochemistry and genetics. As a result, their powers of agricultural manipulation were limited. Chickens ran around pecking worms out of the ground. Cows were kept, ten or twenty to a barn, and grazed during the day. If an entrepreneurial peasant had chosen to lock a thousand chickens inside an airless coop, the result would have been a deadly bird flu that probably would have wiped out the chickens and the villagers—no doctor, shaman or priest would have been able to prevent it.

But modern science knows the secrets of animal disease. Vaccinations, antibiotics and pesticides supported the technological advances that gave us automatic feeders and air-conditioning systems. We were suddenly able to cram tens of thousands of chickens in tiny coops and produce eggs and meat with chilling efficiency.

We could do this thanks to the scientific study of animals, which looked at animals not as sentient beings, but as commodities—there to be managed and manipulated for our benefit, not theirs.

Our technological advances allowed us to intensively farm animals with little risk to ourselves, or at least so it seemed to begin with. Some say this was a critical moment, which enabled us to "feed the world."

- We were able to cross breed seeds to create plants that produced higher yields or were resistant to the latest pesticides and herbicides.
- We could forget about crop rotation and spray the soil with chemical fertilizers instead.
- We could create larger and larger animal farms, using grains and antibiotics to make animals bigger, while minimizing the space they needed to live and to eat.
- We became a caricature of God, behaving as though the natural world and the animals in it were mere commodities whose sole purpose is to serve us.

The march of history had clouds gathering on the horizon. We'll get into these in the next chapter.

SUBSIDIES: THE GAME CHANGER

Why has the meat industry got so big and powerful since the Second World War? How did we get from the quintessential farmer with his three cows, to feedlots where ten thousand cattle are fattened on a diet of grains and soy?

The most succinct answer is government subsidies. Simply put, your taxes are being used to prop up the animal industry, sell us a lie, and drive the illusion of cheap meat.

It can be jarring that I grew up within the same industry that I am now fighting. I have flashbacks and remember hearing updates on subsidies, and it's the broader political scene that supported us. I took it as standard that subsidies were an integral part of the system and required to feed the world.

So when I started investigating the murky world of government farm subsidies, I was appalled and angry. I think you will be too!

SO WHAT EXACTLY IS A SUBSIDY?

A subsidy is a financial grant, funded by public tax money, and offered by the government to private businesses or public institutions. Its purpose is to reduce production costs so the industry receiving the subsidy is in a better financial position.

Subsidies to the agriculture industry are important yet rarely talked about. The argument is they are useful for protecting a nation's food supply, particularly supporting farmers through unforeseen events, like extreme weather. However, not all subsidies are positive.

What if I told you that your tax money provides **one million dollars every minute** to prop up agriculture? And it isn't going to small-scale farmers. Most subsidies go to large animal farms and mono-crops like soybean and corn, which are used to feed cattle. Meanwhile, only 1% of this amount goes towards measures that could help protect the environment from the detrimental impact of animal farming.[9]

THE REAL PRICE OF MEAT

> According to studies, the US government spends up to $38 billion every year subsidizing the meat and dairy industries. Less than 1% of that sum is allocated to fruit and vegetable production.[10]

So we have a system where our tax money—which should be used for public services and to support its citizens and the environment—is being used to drive down the price of meat. As we'll see in the next chapter, meat has a lot to answer for when it comes to ecological collapse, social issues, chronic disease and zoonotic viruses—not to mention the suffering of billions of animals every year.

This is increasingly a pressing question and one that isn't discussed enough. We hear governments all over the world telling us there's no money for welfare, no money to abolish homelessness, not enough funding available for education, free healthcare, and climate protection. Yet at the same time, governments continue to make extravagant handouts to the meat industry. This means that all of us, regardless of our lifestyle choices, end up contributing to animal farming and all its consequences.

In Europe, subsidies are so huge that each head of cattle gets a subsidy worth $2.20 per day.

This means that a European dairy cow's annual income is higher than half the world's population.[11]

And of course, the cow isn't benefiting from this, the meat industry is.

In the UK, 90% of the annual profit of livestock farmers comes from government subsidies.
For comparison, only 10% of the annual profit of fruit farmers comes from subsidies.[12]

In the US, animal farmers were awarded $12 billion in subsidies in 2018 and $16 billion in 2019.[13] At the same time, $5 billion was cut from social programs like food stamps.

Globally, we're eating more meat than ever before. Whereas the average per capita consumption of meat was around 50 pounds (23 kilos) per person in 1961, this had almost doubled to 95 pounds (43 kilos) per person in 2014.[14] In the US, per person consumption of meat averages at 273 pounds (124.1 kilos) per year, up 40% since 1961.[15] It's not just that more meat is being produced. We have also been sold the idea that meat is good for us.

Meat has always been something aspirational. Once only the richest people could afford to slaughter an animal for food. Meat was a symbol of prosperity. Henry IV of France is said to have made the impractical promise of "a chicken in every pot." I say impractical because the infrastructure simply was not available to make it possible. It wasn't possible until technological advances meant farmers could grow bigger animals, kill them more efficiently, and preserve the flesh. That's when meat became both available and affordable in every port.

There was a sort of psychological tipping point after the Second World War, a kind of "beef madness." Soldiers were sent to war with rations of tinned meat. When the war ended, what better symbol of a new world than a sizzling steak? From an unattainable luxury, meat became the new daily bread. Now, we feel entitled to eat meat three times a day if we so wish. And we are still locked into an old way of thinking that associates meat with prosperity, progress, and even health.

Still, something doesn't quite add up. In early times, people could not afford meat but could afford vegetables or they grew their own. Now this has been turned on its head. We live in a world where a hamburger costs pennies, while vegetables, particularly those grown organically, are almost prohibitively expensive.

Logically, this makes no sense. After all, it takes more resources to produce meat. The animal has to be born, then kept alive for years before being killed and processed. It needs to be fed, watered, medicated, transported from feedlot to slaughterhouse, from slaughterhouse to meatpacking plant, etc. Whereas a carrot is just a seed planted in soil that grows over a few months, then it is picked. A carrot does not need to be fed 25 pounds of grain a day, as is the case for cows. Clearly, not all the costs are being carried forward into the price of the final product.

So, how does it work?

Meat is big business and it is profitable. But what if this profit is artificial? What if meat only makes good business sense because government subsidies are propping it up?

Well, guess what? It is.

A lot of your tax money goes straight to big agriculture to keep meat prices artificially low.

FOOD DISPARITY[16]

Price of a hamburger in a fast food outlet: $0.99
Price of a 16-ounce pack of organic kale: $4.56

Price of 5 pounds of chicken drumsticks in Walmart: $4.76
Price of 1 pint of organic blueberries in Walmart: $4.16

It's easy to see which products we are being encouraged to buy.

LOBBYING

When we see the price of meat, dairy, and eggs and think they are cheap, the truth is their price does not reflect reality. For the price to be so low, tax money has been diverted from other, worthier, causes, either social or environmental. This is how you can pay $5 for a tray of blueberries, while a burger can cost you as little as $0.99.

This kind of price-fixing is one of the reasons the meat industry is so profitable and so huge, but there are other reasons too. The industry itself drives business by keeping us coming back for more. Its ties to government mean it can change the nutrition narrative to make animal products seem an essential part of a balanced diet.

A perfect example of how this works is to look at the tobacco industry.

In 2000, a World Health Organisation document reviewed formerly secret internal tobacco industry documents and found evidence of a fifty-year conspiracy to resist smoking restrictions and restore smoker confidence.[17] Tobacco lobbyists did this by spreading misinformation and buying scientific experts to create controversy or to question established facts (including studies whose statistics could be manipulated to show that smoking did not increase the risk of lung cancer). They also pre-empted strong legislation by suggesting instead voluntary codes and weaker laws, not to mention corrupting public officials.

These documents demonstrate that the industry's goal was not to act ethically and responsibly towards consumers and their health, but rather to protect its profits at all costs. It sounds a lot like what the meat industry is doing—funding campaigns to restore consumer confidence and promoting a narrative that disputes the effects of meat on climate change.

These days, it is unlawful to advertise tobacco products.

"The sausage is the cigarette of the future."
CEO of Germany's oldest producer of meat cold cuts[18]

I believe meat is the new cigarette. Meat advertising should go the same way, but we're not there yet. Currently, governments still pay for campaigns that promote meat-eating. More on that in a moment.

When it comes to lobbying, it is not all bad. NGO's (non-governmental organizations) such as Greenpeace, World Wildlife Fund, and Climate Action Network (to name but a few), are busy lobbying the government to fight climate change via ecological farming and changes in policy. The same goes for NGOs pushing for social rights, gender equality, and others. The problem is their budget is a drop in the ocean compared to the billions that the food industry and other corporate interests have at their disposal.

It's David and Goliath, and we need to be championing the underdog.

Part of moving towards a more vegan way of life is to become aware of how our behaviors and thoughts towards animal products are manipulated by an industry that profits from our positive regard.

There are three ways the meat and dairy industry seeks to influence our dietary behaviors. The first is information campaigns, the second is labels, and the third is clever advertising.

INFORMATION CAMPAIGNS
The food industry uses government-funded information campaigns to share the merits of their products, usually in response to opposing campaigns that shine a light on the problematic issues of meat and dairy on health and the environment.

These campaigns are rooted in denial of the problems. Take the environmental aspect, for example. We'll dive into it in the next chapter, but suffice it to say that scientists agree our current meat-centric diet is unsustainable. Instead of acknowledging their part in this, the industry pretends there's no problem.

The same goes for the health element of eating animal products. Information campaigns focus on meat's health benefits, in complete opposition to the many studies that show eating meat increases the risk of chronic disease. For example, the World Health Organization's report on meat and cancer (again, we will look at this more closely in the next chapter).

A good example of pro-meat campaigning is the European Union's 2020 "Proud of EU Beef" campaign, which was funded by 3.6 million euros of public money and incited European citizens to increase their consumption of meat.[19] This campaign was not based on science, but rather aimed to "highlight the benefits of the product" and "make the consumer feel identified and supported in its choice," adding that "consumers who choose to eat red meat should feel at ease should they wish to reaffirm their choice for this product."[20] The question that springs to mind is why should consumers be targeted in this way when the evidence points to meat production being incompatible with the EU's climate targets? Interestingly, the EU's European Green Deal, designed to reduce greenhouse gas emissions by at least 55% by 2030, fails to mention agriculture on its list of proposed policies.[21] This highlights how the political sphere is willingly deaf to the warnings of science.

This is not only an EU problem but a global one. In the United Kingdom, the British Meat Processors Association launched a new website in 2020 aimed at debunking information that encourages consumers to reduce their meat intake, with a particular focus on promoting the "environmental benefits of eating beef and other animals."[22] In 2021, the UK's Agriculture and Horticulture Development Board (AHDB) spent £1.5 million of public money to fund their "Eat Balanced" campaign, a partnership between the pork, beef, lamb, and dairy sectors (which doesn't sound super balanced to me). The AHDB's head of marketing made no secret about what this campaign was about: *"We wanted to create a campaign that feels uplifting and reassuring for consumers who are increasingly being told by the media to reduce their meat and dairy consumption."* [23]

There you have it: this is about reassuring the public that eating meat is absolutely fine, regardless of the truth.

And when it comes to dairy? I think most of us can remember the "Got milk?" campaign, all those famous faces with their milk-taches, looming huge on billboards, extolling the virtues of milk and even chocolate milk as "a high-quality protein was scientifically shown to help repair and rebuild muscles." I wonder what science they are referring to because I'm sure there are healthier post-workout options than a drink filled with sugar, preservatives, and artificial sweeteners. And what about the "Milk Life" campaign, which focused on showing the type of active, happy life you can have when you drink plenty of dairy? The campaign conveniently forgot to mention that this is the very opposite of the life of a dairy cow. It also failed to come clean about the fact that some of the whey and casein proteins in milk have been linked to cancer.[24]

Your tax money funds these campaigns. This money should be used to support people in need, fund green energy infrastructure, and provide social welfare initiatives.

Instead, it is used to help the meat industry promote its products with little regard to their negative effects.

MANIPULATING DIETARY GUIDELINES

But the industry goes further, lobbying for changes to dietary guidelines to keep meat on our plates, even when the research indicates we would be healthier with less. This means that, despite a report by the World Health Organisation classing processed meat as a Class 1A carcinogen and red meat as a Class 2A carcinogen, meat remains a government-approved dietary staple, and people are encouraged to have at least two to three portions of animal foods every day. Perhaps it doesn't come as a huge surprise, since the USA's dietary guidelines are written up by the United States Department of Agriculture in collaboration with the United States Department of Health and Human Services (in that order!).

These dietary guidelines have been issued in the USA every five years since 1985. Interestingly, since that time, has health improved? No. What's wrong with guidelines? It's not that they fall completely short of telling us what's best for us. To some degree, it is common sense that too many processed foods and insufficient exercise contribute to excess weight and chronic disease. And even the "MyPlate" guidance at first appears to offer some reassurance—it tells us to fill half our plate with vegetables and fruits, to focus mostly on whole grains, and to limit sugar.

So far so good. But the problem arises when you dive deeper into the recommendations.

MyPlate is rather vague when it comes to quantities. When we look at the approved "Healthy US-Style Eating Pattern—Amounts from Food Groups," it all becomes much clearer, but not in a good way.

What is interesting is these recommendations have barely changed in the last three revisions of the US Dietary Guidelines (covering 2010–2025). A huge fanfare is made each time about new recommendations and their health implications, but the truth is they are still pushing the type of diet where meat and dairy take pride of place.[25]

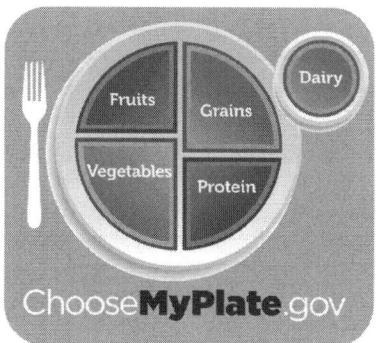

FOOD GROUP: PROTEIN

Amount recommended: 5.5 oz (156 grams) per day from meat, poultry, eggs, fish, nuts, seeds, and soy products.

Problem: Despite telling people to "vary their protein source", the guidance fails to give people the proper information to do so without reverting to animal products. It does so firstly by not including beans and legumes as protein foods (they are in the "Vegetable" food group instead, which leads to confusion), secondly by promoting "meats, poultry, eggs" as the preferred source of protein, and thirdly by recommending a weekly intake of 26 oz (737 grams) of meat, poultry and eggs, 8 oz (227 grams) of fish, and just 5 oz (142 grams) of nuts, seeds and soy products.

FOOD GROUP: VEGETABLES

Amount recommended: 2.5 cups per day

Problem: They've unhelpfully included beans and legumes in the vegetable category, which means they do not appear in the protein category, where they actually belong.

FOOD GROUP: DAIRY

Amount recommended: 3 cups per day

Problem: Recommending that people eat more dairy than vegetables is highly flawed and doesn't match the MyPlate guidance at all. What happened to fill at least half your plate with vegetables?

LABELS

Labels and packaging are another way the meat industry keeps us coming back for more. Clever wordplay and misleading classifications—such as "ethically sourced", "natural", and "humanely raised" on product packaging—often has little to do with the way the animals were raised, and more to do with making the product appear as reassuring and appealing as possible. The same goes for quaint images of farmers in dungarees and happy cows in lush green fields. Take a look at the box section in **Appendix 1** to see examples of labels you might come across and what they really mean.

ADVERTISING

Big business makes a significant effort to understand the mentality that drives consumption. The meat industry is no different, but it has to work even harder in the face of the mounting evidence against it. Marketing is an art form and a science that has been fine-tuned and refined for a century. Adverts, infomercials and campaigns are carefully designed to press certain buttons and get us to buy whatever is being sold. They either target our fears or stimulate our desire, then present their product as a solution or antidote.

When it comes to advertising animal products, the industry relies on our natural desire to fit in, our need to feel we're doing the best for our bodies and the comfort we derive from cultural traditions. Check out the box section in **Appendix 2** to learn how the industry manipulates our wants to sell us their products.

SO, WHY IS THE MEAT INDUSTRY STILL SO POWERFUL?

It isn't just the industrialization of our food supply and advances in science that have allowed this industry to grow. The largest producers of meat and dairy have also had a hand in making sure they receive substantial government subsidies that make their business profitable, even in the face of decreased interest and increased environmental costs. What's more, they manipulate nutritional guidance policy to keep their products firmly on our plates. At the same time, they fund studies and run ad campaigns designed to reassure consumers into buying products that are bad for health and bad for the planet.

They are using tactics last used by the tobacco lobby in the 70s and 80s. As Chapter 3 will show, these are survival tactics by an industry that knows it is no longer tenable.

MEAT THE FUTURE

U.S.   INTERNATIONAL   CANADA   ESPAÑOL   中文

The New York Times

Business   Opinion   Tech   Science   Health   Sports   Arts   Books   Style   Food   Travel   Magazine   T Maga:

The End of Meat Is Here

If you care about the working poor, about racial justice, and about climate change, you have to stop eating animals.

26   May 21, 2020

The future of food is at a tipping point, and the next agricultural revolution is upon us. It is an eventuality that is complex and critical and deserves much more debate and thought. It's so unsettling that we are collectively putting our heads into the sand. In the near future, you will be able to walk into your local supermarket and choose between 3 types of meat: plant-based meat, cell-based meat, and old fashioned animal-based meat.

The meat industry is powerful, but there's a storm gathering on the horizon, and ironically enough, it is made of meat—cell-based meat. Could this new product marry our cultural taste for meat with a production method that bypasses animal suffering and environmental pollution? At first glance, lab-grown meat seems the perfect solution, but many questions hang over this controversial revolution, both ethical and practical.

I do love the rebranding of lab-grown or cell-based meat as "clean meat" as it infers that old-fashioned, animal-based meat is somehow dirty and, therefore inadvertently, we are making the masses accept the political position of veganism!

I have found it a very divisive issue within our vegan community. Some in my large international Facebook group say they wouldn't feed it to their (vegan) dogs! Others seem anxious that veganism will become obsolete once this technology takes over the food systems. There may even be a sense of anger or failure that this technology will lead to the radical changes that the animal rights movement failed to achieve. In contrast, others see it as a way to make everyone vegan without even changing their habits.

THE HISTORY OF THE FUTURE OF MEAT

Cell-based or lab-grown meat is an exciting emerging technology that uses lab-grown animal cells to create meat products, without animal slaughter or resource waste. Stem cells are placed in bioreactors that trick them into growing strands and muscle fibers that combine to create a piece of meat biologically identical to the meat tissue from the original animal. Fat and other ingredients can then be added to give the meat texture that matches traditional meat.

It began in Maastricht, The Netherlands, where a burger was created from cultured cells. At the time, it was only intended as a proof of concept[27] and cost 250,000 euros[28] —that's one expensive burger!

In the last five years, the sector has grown from almost nothing to over fifty companies all racing to bring lab meat to supermarket shelves. It is still a specialized product and expensive to make, but it won't be long before it reaches restaurants and supermarkets.

In December 2020, Singapore authorized the first sale of cultured meat. In fact, there is a restaurant where you can eat cultured chicken made by the Californian start-up Eat-JUST.[29] According to forecasts, the lab meat market will be worth 11.13 billion dollars by 2041.[30] Could it spell the end of traditional meat production? I certainly hope so.

I appreciate how it is both exciting and scary. Potentially, our relationships with animals, the earth, and food are about to change forever. On a purely practical level, it has the potential to save billions of sentient lives a year and help avert the ecological collapse of our planet. It's big stuff at play!

Although conflicted, I have an issue with clean meat because it props up the status quo mentality by perpetuating the myth that animal products are intrinsically desirable or necessary for humans. That is something the vegan and animal rights movements have been challenging since the ancient Greek philosophers. And there are other areas where we should be having a wider debate. Clean meat is not the perfect solution it is often promoted as. The labs themselves require a lot of electricity, which means carbon emissions unless they can be powered by wind, solar, or other green alternatives. And the product itself cannot be said to be completely animal-free, because the stem cells need to be harvested from a donor animal. They can be harvested painlessly, but even so, lab meat cannot strictly be classified as vegan.

But does this mean we should reject it completely or judge those who want to try it? Let's remember that veganism is about choosing more compassionate options. Lab meat, given that it does not necessitate the slaughter of an animal, is a cruelty-free option. It may not be perfect, but it goes a long way to helping us move away from an industry responsible for so much damage and suffering.

Some predict that we may soon live in a less divided post vegan/ animal agriculture world. If 'clean meat' takes over from traditional animal farming, will this mean the end of veganism? Personally, I don't think clean meat will stop the growth of veganism as there are still many ethical and environmental concerns with the production of cell-based meat. And I don't think it will take away the idea of a plant-based diet being better for us than meat-based—just look at all the elite athletes transitioning to plant-based and that has nothing to do with the animals and how they are treated and culled. It is purely about nutritional values and enhanced performance.

My thoughts are that clean meat will provide an easy transition for current meat-eaters, alleviate the unease or cognitive dissonance, save the lives of millions of animals, and reduce the waste that the industry produces. Additionally, it should remove all the drugs used in the current intensive animal industry, which eventually end up on our plates. But it still faces the greatest hurdle—scalability and price.

Once clean meat takes off on an industrial scale (and surely this is something that the meat industry should be spending their billions on!), then a huge number of the ecological issues will also be resolved, or will at least be well on the way to resolution. Finally we can bring our habitation of the planet back into unity rather than opposition. Surely that has to be a win-win for all of us. Could we end up with a compassionate vegan world, but just not as we imagined it?

Our taste for meat is not hard-wired but a practice we are taught from birth. Eating meat is normalized and (literally) rammed down our throats from childhood. It's an unspoken belief system that is all-pervasive and powerful. Indeed, in a perfect world, this is what needs to change, the conditioning, not new ways to produce meat to make it 'clean'.

We are being sold this new technology as an easy way out of the mess we created over the last century. But these claims by cell-based meat can be solved more efficiently by simply reducing our meat consumption. That is the crux of the issue: harnessing our cultural appetite for meat, not mastering new technologies. By simply embracing vegan values we could help solve most of these modern threats and change the world.

Ultimately, I am a vegan realist. I appreciate how increasingly seductive this technology will become. But I still worry that we shouldn't take the quick-win and rely on technology to solve all our problems. Where will it all end, with the ever-increasing consumption of lab-grown meat? With us never needing to learn and evolve? Sometimes we need to challenge ourselves, look inwards, and make lifestyle changes in order to do the right thing and live a life in harmony with the planet that sustains us.

If nothing else, let's at least say we did our best, made our voices heard, and made the world a better place for future generations.

That's the *REBEL VEGAN* way!

3

REBEL WITH A CAUSE

THE DRIVING FORCES ON YOUR VEGAN JOURNEY

There is a driving force more powerful
than steam, electricity and nuclear power: the will.
Albert Einstein[1]

I have already mentioned that we are not just another vegan book. And there are dozens of books on this topic. I should know, I've read most of them! They're helpful, but they're missing something: a deep dive into the why! For any long-term change, there must be a solid foundation of understanding. We need to fully grasp the different values, or driving forces, that support our determination to change our behavior and create a better world. Knowledge is power and it's vital for lasting change!

The reality of our food systems and what is happening under our noses might both disturb and alarm you. It can get ugly, so it's natural to turn away and ignore it. In order to cope, most of us stick our heads in the sand, or look the other way. I did for most of my life. This avoidance is a natural response to having to exist within a system that creates immense injustices on all levels—animal, environmental, and societal. But there comes a point when something pierces our blissful ignorance. It could be a chance conversation with another vegan. It could be a news report about the Amazon rainforest being wilfully burnt down. It could be getting a diagnosis that forces a lifestyle rethink. It isn't easy when our accepted beliefs are shaken up and challenged, but if we want to change, if we want to create a better world, we need to go deeper to understand how certain foods get on our plate and their impact on the wider world.

Being a *REBEL VEGAN* means being bold and brave enough to take this deeper dive. To open yourself up to facing the truth and start this important journey.

Underpinning the standard Western diet[2] is an unspoken ideology that meat is natural, normal and healthy, even necessary. We grow up with and are indoctrinated into this belief system, and only occasionally question it. Increasingly over the last few years, the animal industry has made the headlines in a significant way. There was Cowspiracy's exposé of beef's environmental impact in 2014, the World Health Organization's Meat and Cancer report in 2015, David Attenborough's Blue Planet series in 2017. But these stories follow the same cycle. The information comes out, making the farmers angry, and the animal activists and environmentalists happy. Then there follows a day or two of commentary which makes good viewing for news channels, as they pit these two sides against each other in heated debates. And then.... nothing. We put our heads back in the sand, and carry on with life. The supermarket aisles remain full of beef, rainforests continue to be torn down to plant cattle feed, meat packing plants continue to be manned by exploited workers and meat continues to be promoted as a staple of a healthy balanced diet.

What is the standard American diet (SAD) / standard Western diet?

SAD, also known as the standard Western diet, is a pattern of eating generally characterized by high intakes of meat, dairy products, eggs, fried foods, refined grains, and refined sugars, with low intakes of vegetables, fruits, whole grains, legumes, nuts and seeds.

Having said that, these continuous warnings and alarming reports touch a nerve with some people, and they want to be part of the change. The animal industry is so pervasive and impacts our personal and social lives, and indeed our very survival on Earth. For that reason, the driving forces that bring people to question this unspoken belief system or ideology are many. This is what we will explore throughout this chapter.

What is your driving force for dipping your toe into veganism? We all have one. What originally brought me to veganism was a health scare. For others, it is about animal welfare. For you, it might be that you want to leave a safe, green and thriving world for your children and grandchildren. Whatever it is, it's something that made you stop dead in your tracks and think: wait a second—maybe I don't want to do this anymore. Maybe there is a better way.

That's why knowledge is powerful. Knowledge is the first step. It gives you the motivation to make changes and choices that are really aligned with your ethics and values.

I believe that the survival of our inner and outer environments depends on us weaving veganism into our lives. When it comes to human health, animal welfare, the planet, our water, soil and air, few things are worse than eating meat. It's an uncomfortable truth, but the mountain of evidence is growing every year and becoming indisputable. This chapter will break down exactly why. Get ready to push aside all the increasingly desperate industry-funded "studies" that confuse and misinform, and instead dive into the driving forces that can inspire a healthy vegan life.

Disclaimer: These next chapters are not always a comfortable read. I appreciate these chapters can challenge or disturb, but this knowledge can also change your life. I've tried my best to be concise: to give as much information as needed without being gory (I am vegan, so I'm never going to beat a dead horse!). It will be life-changing, but also confronting (it was for me too) so fasten your seatbelts.

While I am mindful not to use shock tactics, I also don't want to be over-protective or condescending. You deserve better. My aim is to give the most relevant, up-to-date information on each driving force so that you can stand proud as a *REBEL VEGAN*, and go out into the world feeling confident in your lifestyle choices.

The first driving force is animal welfare, and the question this section will answer is, Is it really that bad? Maybe not. This then begs the question of why there's been such a flurry of so-called Ag-Gag laws passed around the world in recent years (we'll dive into this in a second). I will say for now that if slaughterhouses and feedlots had glass walls, we would all feel very differently about meat. This topic is particularly challenging and can be divisive, but can also motivate and inspire the strongest drive for change.

The second is our planet, and the question: Since we've eaten meat throughout the ages, why is it suddenly an ecological problem? I have brought together the most respected research to detail how intensive animal agriculture impacts our air, our land and our oceans.

The third is our health: Is the meat industry really having that big of an impact on our individual and global health? Alarming increases in lifestyle-related diseases like diabetes, obesity and heart disease, as well as the rise of medicine-resistant superbugs and the creation of zoonotic viruses, put our wellbeing in danger from all angles.

The fourth driving force is our society: What does intensive animal farming have to do with social welfare? It's a question that came up when I began researching this book and exploring how we are growing millions of tons of grains, and yet almost three billion people are either going to bed on an empty stomach or facing food insecurity.[3]

In the next four chapters, I have brought together the most current and compelling research to inspire lasting change. Depending on where you are in your vegan journey, you may or may not want to read all of this information chronologically or in one sitting. That's fine. I designed the following driving forces chapters so you can dip in and find what resonates, moves, and motivates you to make a change. Sometimes the truth hurts, but please do push yourself. In my experience, you discover who you really are when you push yourself to the edges of your comfort zone. Living authentically is worth the initial unease/ discomfort.

Let's fasten our seat belts and start this journey.

"We are rebels for a cause, poets with a dream, and we won't let this world die without a fight."
Nobel Prize winner Albert Camus[4]

4

LIVESTOCK
ANIMAL WELFARE

"One day the absurdity of the almost universal human belief in the slavery of other animals will be palpable. We shall then have discovered our souls and become worthier of sharing this planet with them."
Martin Luther King Jr

"Veganism was the next logical extension of Martin Luther King, Jr's, philosophy of non-violence"
Coretta Scott King, activist and widow of MLK Jr[1]

FARMBOY VEGAN

This has been one of the most difficult chapters to research and write, not just because of having to review gruesome details, but because I feel as though I am betraying my background. I feel an element of guilt. After years of denial, I had to confront my family's business and my heritage.

To most intents and purposes, my childhood had something idyllic about it. I grew up in the Canadian countryside. There was a brook at the bottom of the family farm where my grandmother and I would fish. I drove a tractor before I drove a car. I was surrounded by fields dotted with beautiful black and white Holstein cows. It was like living in a children's book. But some of the story was unsuitable for young readers.

Only today can I step back and understand the suffering. And I suppose I suffered from my own cognitive dissonance.[2] I remember staring into the calves' big eyes, stroking the soft fringe between their ears, watching in delight as they played and cuddled together, and the funny way they loped around the field on legs they were still learning to coordinate. I also remember helping to cut off the bulls' testicles, driving to a slaughterhouse, hearing the orphaned calves crying all night.

Once I worked for a neighbouring farmer and had to clean out the chicken sheds. Every so often a hen would escape. Instead of opening up the top hatch of the long row of battery cages and risking more chickens escaping, the neighbour would grab the free bird by its neck, rip its head off with his bare hands and throw it on the manure pile. It may seem shocking, but my child's eyes quickly accepted it. It was just part of life on the farm.

I have immense respect for my family's hard work. My ancestors came to Canada from Scotland, cleared the land, and built up the farm through five generations. They cared deeply for their animals. My grandfather would be up before dawn every morning to feed and look after the cows. If an animal was poorly, he would stay up all night with it. Lucky, the dog would round up the cows twice a day for milking, and their straw was changed every night.

Once, my Dad raced home because one of our horses was pregnant and struggling to deliver her foal. He was so concerned to get back that he broke the speed limits and didn't even stop for the police, who put on their sirens and chased him all the way back to the farm. He sped around our house, jumped out of the truck, raced into the barn, and delivered the new foal all while the perplexed police called in backup and started a stakeout to surround the barn.

I saw farming at its best; my ancestors were proud farmers who loved their land and animals. But alongside this devotion was an assumption that these animals were there to provide for and serve us. Our animals were valued, but they were commodities. They were "livestock," animals regarded as an asset.

I feel a real sense of conflict writing this book, especially this chapter. I grew up entrenched in the mindset that this was the natural, normal order of things. I lived and breathed this belief system. The abuse didn't register as such, it was just the way things were. It was only later, after I experienced the health benefits of a plant-based diet and began doing the research, that everything caught up with me and it all suddenly felt so wrong. I no longer wanted to be part of it. I became a *REBEL VEGAN* for life!

My family's farm was a traditional, family-run, mixed-use farm. They raised crops, the cows grazed in the fields and slept on straw in big wooden barns. But I've noticed something these days when I make my trips home. Over the years, industrial farms have replaced these types of farms. When I drive through the country of my childhood, I don't see cows grazing. The fields are empty of life. The old barns are unloved and falling apart. Instead, I see the huge, prefabricated sheds that house livestock in hidden and unimaginable conditions.

How animals are treated on industrial farms is one of the most urgent ethical questions we face today. Over 77 billion sentient beings—animals with emotions, feelings and consciousness—live and die in the name of protein every year. [3]

THE REAL VICTIMS OF HISTORY

"Non-violence leads to the highest ethics, which is the goal of all evolution. Until we stop harming all other living beings, we are still savages."
Thomas A. Edison[4]

This section is not about trying to shock. It is about finding truth and justice. It's about doing the right thing. When we think about historical crimes, we always think of atrocities inflicted by humans on other humans. What about animals? Are they not the main victims of history and human progress?

It isn't just that humans bring animals to life simply to kill them—it is that humans cause them unimaginable suffering throughout their short lives. They are classed as livestock and have become product units in a profit-driven business. They are no longer individuals.

WHAT IS A SENTIENT BEING?

In Buddhism, a sentient being is a being composed of the five skandhas (or aggregates): matter, sensation, perception, mental formations, and consciousness. The concept of being and being conscious implies these five parts.[5]

Philosophers first coined the word sentience in the 1630s to describe an ability to feel. In modern Western philosophy, sentience is the ability to experience sensations (including light, darkness, pain and pleasure, as well as emotions like love, or suffering).[6]

One of the main excuses for the mistreatment of animals is that they are inferior: not as intelligent as humans, not as conscious, not as complex or refined. This thinking is flawed, and it is rooted in beliefs that put man above all other things. The truth is that humans would be nowhere without animals, or without nature—we should cherish, support and maintain them. As it stands, we treat both as commodities there to be profited from. One way we commodify—and disconnect from—animals is by giving them different names. Chickens become poultry. Cows become cattle. Calves become veal. Pigs become pork. This helps us distance ourselves from the living, breathing being that died to end up, cellophane-wrapped and sanitized, on the supermarket shelf.

Animals are sentient beings. All religions recognize this to a degree, and the Greek philosophers we mentioned earlier knew it too. We have reconfirmed it scientifically, in modern times. The Cambridge Declaration, written by a group of well-respected, prominent neuropharmacologists, neuro-physicists, neuro-anatomists and computational neuroscientists, was signed on 7th July 2012 and attests to that. The declaration states that the absence of a neocortex (the part of the brain in humans attributed with complex thinking, like language) does not stop an animal from experiencing affective states such as love, pain, compassion, fear and even shame.

Evidence shows that animals have the neural capabilities to experience conscious states, as well as the capacity to exhibit intentional behaviors. Anyone who has had a pet or even interacted with one, or has observed animals in their natural habitats, knows this to be true. However, most of us go through life with this cognitive dissonance between our natural inclination to love animals and our tradition of eating them.

Animals are conscious, intelligent beings with complex social and emotional needs. These needs cannot be met in a factory farm setting. The goal in these places is simply to get them from birth to slaughter and extract maximum revenue from them as efficiently as possible. They are treated as a product, rather than a living, breathing being. If this sounds like a dystopian horror show, that's because it is.

Here's what the agricultural revolution gave humans: the systems, drugs and scientific know-how to keep animals alive while ignoring their psychological, emotional, and social needs. Vaccinations, medications, antibiotics and hormones, pesticides, automatic feeders, automatic milking machines—all these make it possible to cram thousands of animals together in a tiny space to produce meat, eggs and dairy with horrifying and brutal efficiency.

But is it really that bad? When we soul-search, we have to admit that we do not want to inflict physical pain on another creature, so we shy away from the images that this throws up for us. Our desire to turn away from the truth is in part what makes it possible for these things to take place under our noses. We grow up with rose-tinted spectacles when it comes to what happens on a farm.

I had an animal farm set by Fisher-Price. I remember the little animals with their smiling faces, the little plastic fences, sheds and trees. It was deceptively reassuring to recreate the real farm behind my house into this bright, cheery, genteel world. Big agriculture, or big ag, depends on this. They know that we do not want to think about the pain behind the product, so they hide their practices behind reassuring logos and soothing slogans. But if it was all fine, if there was nothing to hide, nothing to see, nothing to report, then why do we need Ag-Gag laws designed to hide and protect farming practices?[7]

> *"The fate of farm animals is not an ethical side issue. It concerns the majority of Earth's large creatures: tens of billions of sentient beings, each with a complex world of sensations and emotions, but which live and die on an industrial production line."*
> **YUVAL NOAH HARARI, author of Sapiens**[8]

COVER UPS AND TERRORISM ON THE FRONT LINES

Ag-gag laws first came into force in the US in the 1990s, as a way to stop underground activists associated with the Animal Liberation Front movement. They have since spread like wildfire and been enacted in Australia, Canada and many European countries. These laws make it a crime to take photos or videos of an industrial farm without the owner's consent. In 2002, the Animal and Ecological Terrorism Act was enacted to "prohibit entering an animal or research facility to take pictures by photograph, video camera, or other means with the intent to commit criminal activities or defame the facility or its owner." Those found guilty of committing this offence were put on a terrorist registry. What is interesting here is the "defame the facility or its owner" element. To me, this is an admission that what goes on behind the barbed wire of our industrial farms is so wrong and unpalatable that it "defames" the people responsible for it. It is a cover-up and an acknowledgement of guilt.

In 2006, the Animal Enterprise Terrorism Act was passed in the USA, prohibiting any person from any behavior "for the purpose of damaging or interfering with the operations of an animal enterprise," including conduct that could damage or cause "the loss of any real or personal property." An interesting question is about use of the term "terrorism" to describe the acts of passionate activists whose mission, ironically enough, is to shed light on the terror suffered by animals. Whether you agree with their methods or not, these are people who have been unable to turn away from the reality of what is happening in factory farms.

Similarly, in 2019, Australia passed the Right to Farm Bill, which criminalizes anyone who damages property, releases livestock, or encourages others to unlawfully enter animal facilities.[9] It is worth pausing on the bill's title. Nobody is threatening farming in itself, it's the "right" to abuse and slaughter that is being contested. The activists are not taking videos of farmers innocently going about their business of planting carrots or lovingly tending to their animals. In fact, many farmers are shocked when they see the horror show inside factory farms.

The truth is, without undercover reporting, we would have no idea what really happens in these animal facilities. According to the non-profit organization Government Accountability Project, this type of whistleblowing is essential. To suggest that there are proper channels by which "law-abiding" whistle-blowers can report abuse ignores the fact that employees who complain about conditions tend to either be intimidated into silence or fired.[10]

We need to ask, why are our governments supporting the limiting, concealing and suppressing of this information? Do they think we can't handle the truth? Do we not have the right to know how our food is produced? Or is the traditional image of farming so dear to us that we are collectively willing to turn a blind eye?

Let's buckle up and explore what these Ag-Gag laws are actually protecting. What are we not allowed to see? The brief descriptions that follow can be confronting, but I have been mindful not to be gratuitous. My mission is to tell the truth in as respectful a way as possible, while not diluting the facts. It was a tough balance to strike. For the brave, we recommend a deeper dive with the documentary Earthlings (you can find a link to this in the Resources Appendix).

AFO AND CAFO
ANIMAL FEEDING OPERATION AND
CONCENTRATED ANIMAL FEEDING OPERATION[11]

An AFO is a term used by the US Environmental Protection Agency (EPA) to define enterprises where animals are kept and raised in confined conditions.

AFOs process animals, manure, urine, dead animals, and production operations on a small area of land. Animals in AFOs and CAFOs do not graze—feed is brought to them.

*A CAFO is a large AFO,
one with more than 1,000 animal units.*

One animal unit is defined as being equivalent to 1,000 pounds of live animal weight, which equates to:

*1,000 beef cows,
700 dairy cows,
2,500 pigs (over 55 pounds each),
125,000 broiler chickens,
OR 82,000 laying hens.*

MEAT THE TRUTH:

*"Animals run no risk of going to hell,
they are there already."*
Victor Hugo of Les Misérables

WHAT REALLY HAPPENS ON MODERN FACTORY FARMS

Farm animals are intelligent, gentle beings with complex personalities and strong social ties. However, today's factory farms do not allow them to express their natural behaviors. Instead, they are mistreated, neglected, and mutilated before being sent to a violent death.

COWS

Cows are consumed as beef and veal, kept as dairy producers, and used for products such as leather and manure. In their natural habitat, cows will live up to 22 years.[12] In the industrial farming industry, dairy cows live on average 4 years, while cows grown for beef are slaughtered after only 18 months.[13]

COWS RAISED FOR BEEF

Cows raised for beef usually start their life on a ranch or farm. Within a few days of being born, male calves will be restrained and a hot iron will be pressed into their flesh to identify them. Their horns will either be gouged out or burnt off. I recall helping with this as a boy and wanting to run away from the cries. They will be castrated, either by ripping or cutting the testicles from the scrotum, or by clamping down on them so they atrophy.

All this is done without pain relief. I vividly remember helping with this procedure on our farm. The bulls were put in a holding pen, and a contraption was used to place a strong elastic band around their scrotum. The band stayed in place until the bull's balls dried up and dropped off. This was done in order to make the bull produce more meat.

After about a year, they are shipped to auction, and then sent— sometimes hundreds of miles away—to feedlots, also known as concentrated animal feeding operations (CAFOs), where they are crowded together by the thousands. Instead of their natural diet of grass and hay, they are fed corn and soy, as well as the remains of other animals (see What Do Factory Farmed Animals Eat box section). This is designed to fatten them up quickly, but places undue strain on their digestive systems. The unnatural feed causes their stomachs to bloat to such an extent that it makes it hard for the cows to breathe. This is worsened by the air quality, which in CAFOs is saturated with ammonia, methane and other gasses from the buildup of animal waste. The fumes cause the cows to develop chronic respiratory conditions.

The squalid, unsanitary and crowded conditions create the perfect breeding ground for bacterial infections, so hormones and antibiotics are used to keep the animals alive and get them to their slaughter weight as quickly as possible. This is less about the animals' health more about profit. They are kept alive but do not experience a life worth living.

Once they have reached their kill weight, cows are sent to slaughterhouses. They are herded into trucks, where they will go without food, water, or rest for the journey, which sometimes takes days. Many will collapse from heat exhaustion. In the winter, cows can freeze to the side of the trucks and have to be pried off with crowbars. When they arrive at the slaughterhouse, many will be too sick to walk. These will have ropes or chains tied to their legs and will be dragged off. The cows that can still move are terrified and do not want to leave the truck. Workers prod them in the face and body with electric prods or beat them with chains to get them to move.

After being unloaded, cows are forced into a pen and shot with a captive bolt gun. This is meant to stun them and render them insensitive to pain. However, the lines move fast and workers are poorly trained, so many cows are still conscious when their throats are cut and are alive for as long as seven minutes after this. One longtime slaughterhouse worker told the Washington Post, "They blink, they make noises. The head moves, the eyes are wide and looking around... They die piece by piece."[14]

COWS RAISED FOR DAIRY

"My oat milk saves all the cows in the yard."

Cows, like all mammals, only produce milk after pregnancy to feed their young. To produce milk for our consumption, cows must give birth to one calf per year. Three months after giving birth, they are artificially inseminated again. If the cow does not conceive after her first insemination, or does not produce enough milk after her first calf, she is sent to slaughter.

If a dairy cow's calf is female, she will spend the first 8 weeks of her life isolated in a small pen before becoming part of the dairy industry. If it is male, he will be shipped to the veal industry, where he will spend 18 to 20 weeks gaining weight in a crate typically no bigger than 22 inches (0.56 meters) wide and 58 inches (1.47 meters) long, where he must lay in his own faeces and urine, before being slaughtered and sold as a delicacy.[15] Regardless of the sex, the calf is taken away from its mother immediately after birth, so that all of her calf's milk can be harvested for human consumption.

Cows are social animals with particularly strong bonds between mother and calf. It has been shown that cows mourn the loss of close friends, just like we do. Surely we can relate and use our imagination to put ourselves in their place for a second? Mothers give birth and see their newborn being taken away crying. These cries can be heard for days. Imagine going through that emotional wrench, and then being hooked up to a milking machine several times a day, until you are artificially inseminated again, only for the cycle to continue. Round and round again until you are so broken, that you're only fit for the slaughterhouse.

Milking when done naturally is not painful. But in industrial dairy farms, it is a different story. A cow naturally produces around 8 liters (2.1 gallons) of milk per day for her calf. Cows in the dairy industry are bred and drugged to produce over double that - 5.2 gallons (20 liters) a day. That puts an incredible amount of strain on their body. To produce just one liter (0.26 gallons or 2 pints) of milk, a cow's body must pump half a ton of blood through her udder. Increasing her milk productivity means the cow suffers. One of the physical ways this manifests is mastitis, a condition where their udders become inflamed and painful.

So what about all those cows we see in the fields, grazing so peacefully? Most of these cows are either beef cattle before they are sent to CAFOs, or young dairy cows before their first calf. Commercial dairy cows live in cramped stalls where they are tied in place. They are unable to walk, turn around, or interact with other cows. Sometimes they are kept in cubicles. The floors tend to be concrete, which is slippery and stressful for the cow to move around on. Their urine and faeces are mechanically removed. They are milked by machines. Their tails are docked without anesthetics to allow for easy access to their udders. They are milked four to five times a day. This pattern is repeated for three to six years, or until the cow no longer produces enough milk. She is then sent to slaughter.

PIGS

A pig's natural lifespan is ten to fifteen years. In the industrial farming industry, they are slaughtered at six months old.[16] Breeding sows are slaughtered after three to four years.[17]

SOWS

Female pigs, or sows, are repeatedly inseminated to give birth. Their litters can be any number of piglets, up to twelve at a time. During their pregnancy and after birth, sows are kept in gestation crates so small that they can barely move or turn around. They eat, urinate, defecate, and give birth in the same tiny space, sometimes so tiny that the bars cut into their skin.

Mother pigs, just like humans and other animals, instinctively want to nurture and teach their young. In nature, sows would have the space, material and time to do so; they typically nurse their babies for 10–17 weeks. But in factory farms, the piglets are taken away from their mother after only three weeks.

Male piglets are castrated by scalpel or knife in the first three days of their life, without pain relief. They are suspended by their hind legs, and the testes are removed by pulling or cutting the spermatic cord. According to meat businesses like Smithfield Foods, this is necessary to "improve the smell and taste of the meat." That's because sexually mature boars (uncastrated pigs) release compounds like skatole and androstenone, which give the meat an unpleasant flavor. Barrows (castrated pigs) can be raised beyond puberty without developing a strong boar flavor, they're also less aggressive, and develop more fatty deposits. So, good for business, but not for the pig. The American Veterinary Medical Association issued a review on the welfare implications of castration in 2013, stating that castration is traumatic for the piglets, who squeal throughout the procedure and lie trembling for days after it happens.[18]

With being kept in confined, unnatural and crowded conditions, pigs develop PTSD—just like humans do when faced with traumatic situations like war or physical trauma. This manifests as compulsive behaviors, one of which is biting their own tails. Instead of giving the pigs more room and better conditions, pork producers perform "tail docking" where they amputate the tail without anesthetic.

Another mutilation pigs go through is "ear notching." Factory farm workers cut notches out of the pigs' right ear to mark which litter they belong to, and cut into their left ear to mark the individual pig's number. Again, no anesthetic is provided.

MALE PIGS

Male pigs are genetically bred and medicated to reach their slaughter weight (250 pounds / 113 kilos) by the time they are just six months old. Due to their weight and lack of space to move, they develop arthritis and struggle to walk or stand. It is not uncommon for pigs to become stuck in their own waste, in dirty feedlots, until such a time as they are shipped to slaughter.

Transport to the slaughterhouse can take up to 28 hours. During this time, the pigs suffer severe overcrowding and extreme temperatures, with no food or water. By the time they arrive, they are exhausted and dehydrated. Many will suffer injuries along the way. Some die before they arrive.

A typical slaughterhouse kills 1,000 pigs an hour. The speed of the slaughter line means many are not properly stunned before their throat is slit. So they can see, hear and smell the pigs around them being killed and dipped into scalding water to remove their hair.[19]

In nature, pigs are extremely clean and social creatures. Scientifically, they have been shown to be just as intelligent as dogs,[20] if not more so. So why is it that dogs live in our homes and become our best friends, while pigs are bred for the sole purpose of becoming bacon? From the day they are born to the day they are killed, pigs, which are sweet, curious and intelligent, endure unimaginable torment and pain. Isn't it time to rethink our relationship with these clever gentle creatures?

CHICKENS

In their natural habitat, chickens will live up to ten years. Factory-farmed chickens live an average of forty-two days.

Ten thousand years ago, chickens were rare birds found in South Asia. They are now global, and are the most widespread domesticated animal in the world. You could therefore argue that chickens are one of the most successful animals on the planet. However, the ghastly trade-off is that they are also the most tortured animal in history.[21] Estimates by the World Economic Forum show that over 50 billion chickens are killed for food every year.[22] This figure does not include male chicks or unproductive hens killed in egg production.

Chickens raised for meat (broilers) and chickens raised for eggs (hens) begin their lives in giant incubators, alongside other chicks. They will never meet their parents. Within days of being born, they are placed beak-first into a machine that cuts off the tip of their beak with a hot blade or a laser. Chicken producers debeak birds to prevent them from pecking at each other, a result of cramped and stressful living conditions.[23]

BROILER CHICKENS

Over the last few decades, broilers have been genetically manipulated to drastically increase the amount of pectoral (breast) and thigh tissue, since these are the most profitable parts of the animal. Unfortunately, this means that these parts grow too fast and too big for their body, which cannot sustain this abnormal growth. They are bred and drugged to gain around 1.76 ounces (50 grams) in weight every day.[24] Their immune systems, organs and legs cannot keep up, resulting in painful bone deformations and congestive heart failure. Some broiler chickens do not make it to the slaughterhouse. They die of thirst because they are physically unable to get to the water. Other causes of death include cancer, over-heating, and infectious diseases.[25]

Broiler chickens are given less than a square foot of space each. Ironically, they get more room in the oven than they ever got while they were alive. They are crammed, 20,000 to 30,000 to each closed broiler shed. These sheds are artificially lit, and computers control the temperature, feeding and watering. Both feed and water are medicated with drugs to control parasites or with antibiotics.

Chickens in the wild tend to live in small flocks of around thirty, with well-defined social hierarchies (this is where the term "pecking order" comes from). They enjoy scratching and pecking for food, taking dust baths, resting and playing together. None of this is possible in a broiler shed. They have no space to roam, they are stressed and tense. Units are only cleaned at the end of each cycle, so within two weeks the floor is covered in waste, and the ammonia fumes become so strong that they burn the birds' eyes. Observers have reported that chickens rub their eyes with their wings and squawk in pain.[26]

After six or seven weeks of these conditions, the broilers reach their kill weight. They are slammed into crates and taken to slaughter. Many sustain broken wings and legs from the rough handling. Many die from the extreme temperatures and stress of the journey. Thanks to automation, slaughterhouses can kill over 8,000 birds an hour using the common method known as live-shackle slaughter. Workers strap the chickens into leg shackles on a moving rail. The birds hang upside down and move along to baths of electrified water, designed to stun them or immobilize them, before moving to a mechanical blade that cuts their throat. After they have bled out, they are plunged into boiling water to remove their feathers. Unfortunately, the speed of the assembly line means many chickens are aware of exactly what is happening to them. Some miss the throat cutting blade and are boiled alive.

EGG-LAYING HENS

For egg-laying hens, the conditions are even harder. The majority are kept in cages that are on average smaller than a sheet of paper (around 67 square inches / 432 square cm—that's just over 8x8 inches / 20x21 cm). For context, a hen needs 72 square inches to stand, and 303 square inches to spread her wings. These cages are piled up on top of each other, in sheds that hold tens of thousands of birds. Waste falls from the top cages to the lower ones, causing the same ammonia burn as for broilers. In nature, chickens have a strong urge to nest. Mother hens carefully tend to their eggs, turning them every few hours and even clucking to them. In chicken sheds, they cannot build a nest for their eggs, the eggs just drop through the wires of the cage. Left to their own devices, chickens lay around 10 eggs a year. In factory farms, they lay 300 a year. To get the hens to produce as many eggs as possible, chicken producers use methods like light manipulation (extended periods of artificial daylight are used to encourage laying) as well as forced moulting, a technique where hens are starved of food and water to force their body to produce more eggs.[27]

In these conditions, hens are unable to exercise. They sit in one position their entire life, with their feet pressing into the wires of the cage, and their wings rubbing against the sides. The constant egg laying leaches calcium from their body, so they develop osteoporosis and broken bones. This is a well-known phenomenon called cage-layer fatigue.

After one or two years, the hens' production decreases, and they are shipped to slaughter, most often to be turned into pet food or animal feed because their flesh is too bruised and battered for anything else. Male chicks born to egg-laying breeder hens are useless to the industry (they cannot lay eggs, and are not bred to grow into heavy broilers for the meat industry), so they are either ground alive, or tossed into bags to suffocate. Four to six billion male chicks are killed this way each year.[28]

In 2003, there was a short spell of outrage in America when a lawsuit was filed against an egg ranch for killing 30,000 hens by dumping them, alive, into a wood-chipper.[29] No charges were brought, because as it happens, this is standard practice in the industry. The Humane Slaughter Act does not cover chickens.[30]

YOUR FANTASY FARM

Fast food companies, supermarkets and meat giants go to great lengths to show you the clean, friendly face of farming. Cue the adverts that depict a farmer in a checked shirt and jean dungarees gently patting a cow's bottom as she walks through a wooden gate onto a lush green field, or a flock of shiny-feathered chickens clucking and pecking in front of a large coop surrounded by trees, or even a farmer milking his cow by hand, into a bucket.

Why? Because you might not eat that hamburger if you knew what the cow had to endure for you to buy meat for 99 cents.

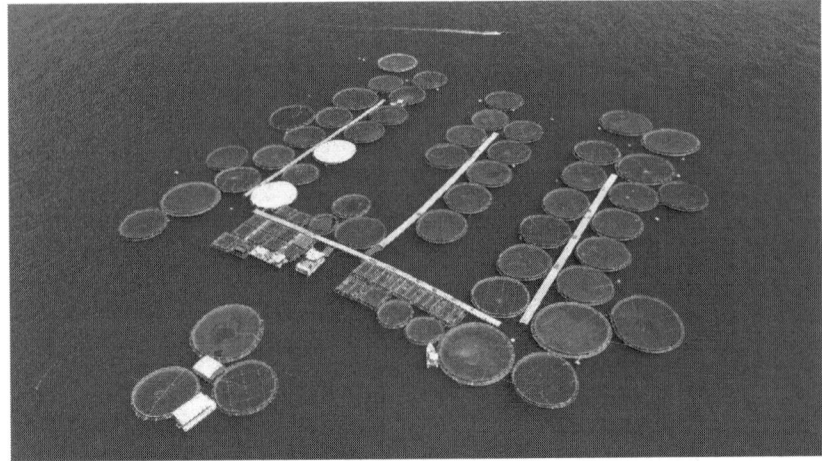

FISH: WATER FARMING

It is shocking for many to learn that fish are just another exploited farm animal. Half of all fish consumed globally come from aquafarms, and this industry is growing three times faster than land-based animal agriculture. This is perhaps a response to our almost exhausted natural fisheries. Aquafarms are like water-based concentrated animal feeding operations (CAFOs). Genetic engineering is used to ensure the fish grow faster and bigger than they would in the wild. In some countries, antibiotics are added to the water or fish feed. Residues of these drugs are present in the end product and on your plate.

Fish farmers cram as many fish as possible into the smallest space possible. Large farms, the size of four football fields, can contain over a million fish. These overcrowded conditions mean that fish cannot navigate properly and keep bumping into each other, causing sores and fin damage. Salmon, which are 30 inches (75 cm) long, are given space equivalent to a bathtub of water each.

Fish are continually sorted by size to ensure that the larger ones are moved to the appropriate size grouping. The process of "grading" involves netting or pumping fish out of their tanks, and dumping them onto grates of varied space gaps to divide them by size. Fish farmers sometimes starve the fish for 24 hours before doing this.

Parasite infestations and diseases are common in fish farms. As many as 40% of farmed fish are blind—this problem is not addressed because it does not cause a loss of profit. Sea lice eat at the fish, causing their scales to fall off which leave large sores. In ocean-based fish farms, sea lice often eat down to the bone.

Many species of farmed fish are carnivorous, so wild fish need to be caught to feed farmed fish. This is incredibly inefficient and unsustainable. It can take one pound of wild fish to produce one pound of farmed salmon or sea bass. Fish farmers sometimes give fish oil and fish meal to algae-eating fish to speed up their growth. They also add chemicals and antibiotics to help the fish survive the harsh conditions in aquafarms. This could be why levels of dioxin and PCB are up to seven times higher in farmed fish than in wild-caught fish.

Similarly to chickens, there are no regulations to ensure that fish are treated humanely. According to PETA, almost 40% of farmed fish die before it is time for slaughter. Those who survive are starved for up to ten days to reduce waste contamination of the water during transport. Common slaughter methods include leaving them to suffocate on ice or in the air, a process that can take more than ten minutes. Other methods include piercing their hearts or cutting off their gills, as well as immobilizing the fish with cold water before killing them with carbon dioxide.[31]

Wild-caught fish do not have to endure life on an aquafarm, but they still suffer fear and pain. It is estimated that one to three trillion fish are wild-caught every year. They are chased to the point of exhaustion by huge trawl nets. Once caught, they are crushed under the weight of other fish. It can take hours, sometimes days, for fish to be captured. During this process, many fish die or become injured. Once caught and landed, the fish are either left to suffocate, or die from processing (such as gutting, filleting, or freezing—all while still conscious).[32]

Cows, pigs, chickens and fish are not the only animals killed for meat. Ducks, rabbits, geese, turkeys, sheep, goats, mice, rats, pigeons, buffalo, horses, donkeys, mules, camels, as well as cats and dogs, are also tortured and killed daily for food.[33] And that's without mentioning the horrors they go through in product testing and medical research industries. That's another story and book in itself!

VOICE FOR THE VOICELESS

"Never, never be afraid to do what's right, especially if the well-being of a person or animal is at stake. Society's punishments are small compared to the wounds we inflict on our soul when we look the other way."
Martin Luther King Jr

If you have read through this section, thank you. It is not easy to examine and accept our involvement in this system and face the reality of today's food system. I too found it a struggle to research and write about billions of animals suffering unnecessarily. I feel that the meat industry depends on us wanting to turn the other way—it depends on us wanting to believe that what goes on in industrial animal farms is natural and even humane. Because the industry knows that if we saw how these animals are treated, most would not want to be part of it. We buy our meat nicely cut up, cleaned and plastic-wrapped in the supermarket, but there is nothing natural or humane about the way animals are bred, genetically modified, and intensively farmed to end up on our plates.

I have made every effort to give you this information in a straightforward and sober way. I was mindful to be factual, not emotive, to avoid shock tactics or gore. However, I would also urge you to be brave and watch the videos. There is nothing like seeing with your own eyes what these animals go through, to really cement your decision to go vegan.

Maybe grab a friend who is willing to go on this journey with you, or a vegan friend, and challenge yourself to look over the walls and fences of factory farms and slaughterhouses. Be open to letting the images change you. Allow yourself to feel that pain, to experience that rising indignation. Smash through those Ag-Gag laws and fluffy marketing to embrace the reality and your feelings. Because if it is unpleasant to watch, that only proves that you are a compassionate human and a budding *REBEL VEGAN*.

Animal welfare is not only about animals. It's about us too. Because if we condone this type of treatment, what kind of message are we sending? Is it okay to treat other conscious beings this way? What kind of world are we accepting, if we accept this sort of everyday normalized violence? If we turn a blind eye to this, what else can we turn a blind eye to?

In a time in history when we are more and more polarized and when politics are getting more extreme, we should be careful about what we accept under the guise of "it's always been like this" or "they're 'only' animals." After all, this is how all oppression starts—by seeing certain beings as inferior to us, or ours to use and exploit. To stop the oppression, we must stop buying into an industry that knowingly tortures our fellow earthlings. This central driving force can empower us all to align our ethics of compassion and justice with a more sustainable and kinder way of living. #voiceforthevoiceless

> *Today and everyday - 200 million land animals are slaughtered in food production.*
>
> *If we were killed at the same rate, the human race would become extinct in 2 and a half weeks.*[34]

5

ENVIRONMENT

INCONVENIENT SCIENCE

"We must either let some eating habits go, or let the planet go. It is that straightforward, and that fraught."
Jonathan Safran Foer[1]

Do you remember "An Inconvenient Truth" (2006), that ground-breaking documentary by Vice President Al Gore? This was the first film that broke down the climate crisis, and it had a real impact on me. I made changes to my lifestyle on the strength of it and fancied myself as a radical eco-warrior. But I was still eating meat, in blissful ignorance of its devastating environmental impact. Thinking back, I can see that while that documentary was powerful and shone a light on the dangers of fossil fuels and some of our modern ways of life, but it also turned a blind eye to one of the biggest factors responsible for pollution and ecosystem collapse—the meat industry.

Perhaps Al didn't want to ruffle the feathers of his friends in Washington. As we have seen, the meat industry has persuasive power and strong links to policy-makers. That being said, Al Gore went vegan in 2012 and has since admitted, "It's absolutely correct that the growing meat intensity of diets across the world is one of the issues connected to this global crisis—not only because of the [carbon dioxide] involved, but also because of the water consumed in the process."[2]

Let's begin with a reality check. It is an uncomfortable reality based on inconvenient science; our current diet and food system is unsustainable. We cannot safeguard our environment for future generations while regularly eating meat. Animal agriculture is responsible for releasing powerful greenhouse gases into the atmosphere, burning down rainforests, and creating ocean dead zones, all of which are speeding up climate change towards a planet that is uninhabitable—not just for other animals, but also for humans.

It's now a classic, but when Cowspiracy hit our screens in 2014, it was radical and groundbreaking. Nobody had been talking about this, certainly not in the mainstream. Suddenly, the implications of animal agriculture for our environment were right in front of our faces, undeniable and frightening.

Being a true *REBEL VEGAN* is about compassion and accepting that the future of our planet is our responsibility. This means going beyond energy saving light bulbs and recycling. We must make daily choices that protect the world we live in.

Climate scientists agree that eating plant-based is the most impactful and positive step we can all take to halt the climate crisis. And it is a step we cannot bypass. According to a report from the Intergovernmental Panel of Climate Change (IPCC), even if we do everything necessary to reduce emissions and halt climate change, we will not meet the Paris Climate Agreement's goals unless we dramatically reduce our reliance on animal products.

This is a sobering thought, and a catalyzing one. Each of us will have two or three meals today, so we can immediately take action in reversing climate change. We can do this simply by switching from meat to plants. The truth is we can all be *REBEL VEGANS* and save the world one meal at a time.

GREENHOUSE GASES

The fact that animal agriculture is a disaster for the environment is not my opinion—it's not even an opinion—it's fact. Despite what certain strident climate deniers will have you believe, our modern lifestyles put incredible strain on our planet. Mother Nature has been whispering her pain for decades. She is now beginning to scream, and we need to listen before it's too late.

Let's begin with greenhouse gas emissions. The greenhouse gas effect is a natural occurrence whereby gases in the atmosphere trap heat from the sun and warm the planet. It is a good thing, because without it, our planet would be a freezing and uninhabitable place. The problem is our voracious burning of fossil fuels is causing the greenhouse gas effect to turn on us.

For almost a million years, the concentration of greenhouse gases has been around 200-280 parts per million (this means that for every million molecules of air, there were 200-280 molecules of greenhouse gases). In the last hundred years, this has jumped to 400 parts per million.[3] This has caused more heat to be trapped in the Earth's atmosphere and as a result global temperatures rise. In turn, this leads to the climate disasters we are seeing today, from soaring temperatures (for example, Canada hit a record 46.1 degrees Celsius / 115 °F in 2021[4]), to record ice melting (for example, Greenland ice sheets lost 8.5 billion tons in melted ice in one day in July 2021— enough to cover Florida in two inches of water[5]), to torrential rainfall, devastating floods and wildfires throughout the world.

Animals in feedlots are the primary source of methane (86 times more powerful than CO_2) and nitrous oxide emissions (310 times more powerful than CO_2). These greenhouse gases are a huge contributor to global warming.

Animal agriculture produces more greenhouse gas emissions than all the transportation sector (that's cars, trains and planes). Can it be true? The UN's Food and Agriculture Organization (FAO) says it is responsible for just 14.5% of greenhouse gas emissions, which makes it sound like animal agriculture is not the most urgent thing to tackle in the fight against climate change.

But a new report shows the FAO's calculations were flawed because they failed to include the negative impact of deforestation due to animal agriculture. With this being considered, animal agriculture is responsible for 87% of greenhouse gas emissions.[6]

Let that sink in for just a moment. Compare it to the 13% caused by other things. From that place, is it more important to buy an electric car, or switch to plant-based eating?

HOW CAFOS (LARGE FACTORY FARMS) POLLUTE THE AIR[7]

Warehouses where animals are kept:
The air pollution in these warehouses is potentially deadly to both animals and humans if the fans stop working. The fans simply blow this contaminated air (which contains ammonia, particulates, feathers and feces) out of the building into the environment.

Animal waste:
CAFO wastes are stored in structures that are neither treated nor aerated. This results in an off-gassing of pollutants when the waste is transported or sprayed onto farm fields.

Waste spreading:
Once or twice a year, the solid waste at the bottom of storage tanks is scraped out and spread onto fields, resulting in even worse air pollution.

Heavy air pollution:
Over 168 different gases are emitted from CAFO waste, including methane, hydrogen sulfide and ammonia.

LAND AND WATER

AN INEFFICIENT USE OF PRECIOUS RESOURCES
Animal agriculture gobbles up the lion's share of resources essential to our survival: land and water. Half of the world's habitable land is used for agriculture. Animal agriculture also accounts for 30% of all freshwater consumption.[8]

Using animals for food is one of the most energy-inefficient ways to eat. After all, the animal needs food and water to grow. In contrast, a plant just needs good quality soil and water. Of the 19.7 million square miles (51 million square km) currently used for agriculture, 77% is used for livestock (this includes grazing land for animals and land used for animal feed production), while 23% is used for crops. Despite taking up such a huge percentage of agricultural land, only 18% of the world's calorie supply comes from meat and dairy.[9]

To put it another way, the land used for crops is four times smaller than the land used for livestock, and yet it supplies more calories for the global population. A sobering thought, but one that provides hope and solutions for the future, if we can listen and learn to change.

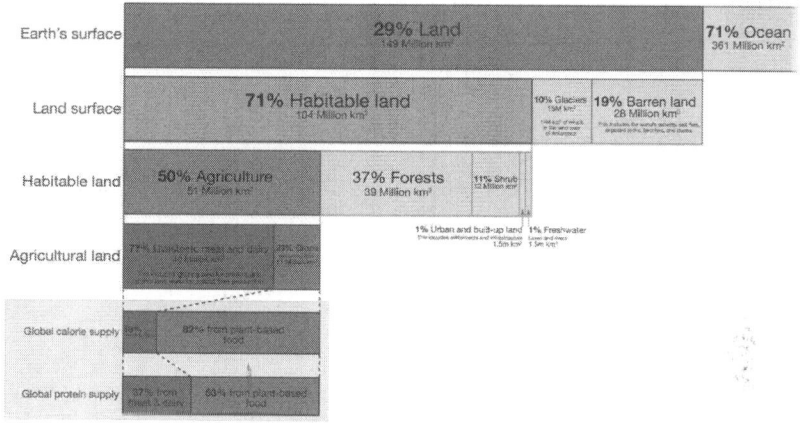

Global land use for food production

https://ourworldindata.org/global-land-for-agriculture

RAINFORESTS DESTRUCTION

We currently have a situation where rainforests are being cut or burnt down to make space for crops grown to feed farm animals to satisfy our taste for meat. The stats are shocking and get scarier by the day. The World Bank asserts that animal agriculture is responsible for nearly 90% of Amazon rainforest destruction[10], with more than 80,000 acres of tropical rainforest[11] and 135 animal, plant, and insect species lost[12] due to this destruction each day.[13] In the last 40 years, 1 billion hectares of rainforest have been destroyed. That's an area the size of Europe. We are losing a football field of forest every single second.[14]

Rainforests are much more than just trees or a trip-of-a-lifetime destination. They are a carbon-storage facility. They are an oxygen factory. They are an Ali Baba's cave of animal and plant species that have yet to be discovered and studied. They are home to indigenous tribes who have lived there for millennia.

Feedlots and grain production for cattle feed are the primary reason for deforestation, and there are two main reasons this must stop. Firstly, burning down trees releases carbon into the atmosphere. Secondly, fewer trees means the planet is less able to absorb carbon (including all that extra carbon we are pumping out because of our modern lifestyles).

Trees are carbon storers or sinks—they absorb CO_2 from the air and store it into their bark. When we burn them, we release all this back into the environment, compounding the global warming issue, and accelerating climate change.

Interestingly, during 2020, when the whole world ground to a halt for Covid, deforestation sped up. 12% more undisturbed tropical rainforests were razed down in 2020 compared to 2019.[15] For the first time ever, the Amazon rainforest emits more carbon dioxide than it absorbs. It used to store the carbon that drives climate change, now it is accelerating climate change.

Two reasons for this. The first is the fires deliberately set to clear land for beef and soy cause emissions. The second is hotter temperatures, and drafts mean the Amazon has become a source of CO_2 rather than a sink.[16] We may have passed the tipping point, or be very close to doing so.

Research from the World Resources Institute shows extreme weather events are on the rise everywhere, including within the rainforests themselves. Even the wetlands are burning. Combine global warming and deforestation, and you have the perfect storm of warmer, drier conditions, making forests even more vulnerable to disease and fire. Burning releases more carbon emissions, which speed up global warming. You can see how we have a vicious cycle on our hands. And the cycle is speeding up, unless we find a way to stop it. The most efficient way to do this is to stop supporting the industry responsible for deforestation.

OUR MOST PRECIOUS RESOURCE:

WATER, THE GIFT OF LIFE, WASTED

Another inconvenient truth is we cannot survive without water. It's the basis of all life. Even if we colonize and build a community on the moon or Mars, they will need to import water. This is our most precious resource. Wars might well be fought over it in the future.

So consider that according to the Stockholm International Water Institute, we will run out of freshwater by 2050 if we continue to produce and eat animal products at the current rate.[17] Given that predictions are for meat consumption to increase, we can assume this date is a best case scenario. So we are facing a situation where the freshwater reserves of the entire planet could be used up in under thirty years.

It sounds unthinkable that we could ever get to this state. But it makes more sense when you break it down and discover that it takes 4,000 gallons (15,000 liters) of water to produce 2 pounds (1 kilo) of beef.[18] Let me put that amount of water into context. It is enough drinking water for one person for 10,000 days (or just over 27 years) if that person drinks the recommended 3 pints (1.5 liters) a day. It took a moment for the significance of this to really sink in. Drinking water for a quarter of a century, or one kilo of beef. No wonder we are running out of clean water.

A question that pops up for me here is, shorter showers for life, or yummy Beyond Burgers?

But animal agriculture doesn't just use unprecedented amounts of freshwater, it also pollutes water—drinking water, rivers, streams and oceans.

WATER FOR MEAT[19]
2 pounds (1 kilo) beef - 4,072 gallons (15,415 liters) of water
2 pounds (1 kilo) goat - 2,315 gallons (8,763 liters) of water
2 pounds (1 kilo) pork - 1,582 gallons (5,988 liters) of water
2 pounds (1 kilo) chicken - 1,142 gallons (4,325 liters) of water
2.1 pints (1 liter) milk - 166 gallons (628 liters) of water

WATER FOR PLANTS[20]
2 pounds (1 kilo) pulses - 792 gallons (3,000 liters) of water
2 pounds (1 kilo) rice - 660 gallons (2,500 liters) of water
2 pounds (1 kilo) bread - 396 gallons (1,500 liters) of water
2.1 pints (1 liter) soy milk - 7 gallons (28 liters) of water
2.1 pints (1 liter) oat milk - 13 gallons (48 liters) of water

OCEAN DEAD ZONES

Across the world, approximately 70 billion animals are farmed for food every year, the majority of them in factory farms, and the numbers keep rising.[21] The waste these animals produce has to go somewhere. The USDA's Natural Resources Conservation Service encourages CAFO owners to "take voluntary actions to minimize potential air and water pollutants from storage facilities, confinement areas and land application areas."[22] This gives the polluters the responsibility to manage—or not—their own waste.

Again, we are expecting big business to police themselves and what we have learned is where there are bucks to be made from animals, corners will be cut and the voiceless suffer. If you think of it from their perspective, animal welfare is a barrier to their profits. Ultimately ensuring animal wellbeing 100% is prohibitively expensive and not a realistic option in the current system.

The latest figures show CAFOs produce 369 million tons of manure, which is thirteen times more than the entire US population. However, human waste is treated via sewer systems and is subject to strict laws to ensure it is processed properly. Animal waste, on the other hand, is stored in open ponds or pits (called lagoons, which make it sound almost pleasant and tropical), and is spread, untreated, onto fields. Let's remember that this is not old-style manure, like I was used to taking directly from the barn to spread over our fields. Those cows had munched on hay and grass all their lives. This is a mixture of animal excrement, antibiotic-resistant bacteria, hormones, bedding waste, antibiotic residues, cleaning and other chemicals, ammonia and even dead animals. It contains a high content of nitrogen and heavy metals, including copper, zinc and lead (due to these being added to animal feed).[23] The only thing between this toxic soup and the environment is a thin layer of clay, which can leak and allow the waste to seep into groundwater.

This untreated waste is also sprayed directly onto fields. The excess runoff ends up in streams and rivers, and eventually the ocean. Because of the chemicals and toxins, it causes an overgrowth of algae. These algae bloom and die off, depleting the oxygen in the water. The result is ocean dead zones—so called because there is no more oxygen left for other lifeforms, which means marine life either asphyxiates and dies, or leaves the area if it can.

Dead zones become oceanic deserts, empty of their usual biodiversity. The planet's largest ever ocean dead zone is located in the Gulf of Mexico and is larger than New Jersey[24], spanning an incredible 8,776 square miles (22,730 square kilometers).

This area has been made completely uninhabitable due to agricultural runoff from the Mississippi floodplain, home to countless pig farms.

And it is likely to keep growing unless we make changes to the food system. The task-force responsible for reducing the dead zone to 1,900 square miles (4,920 square kilometers) has found that a reduction of 60% in waste runoff is required to achieve this goal by 2035.[25] As it stands, there are over 400 ocean dead zones around the globe.[26]

SPECIES EXTINCTION

I grew up surrounded by nature and watching nature documentaries that showed our planet teeming with wildlife. I took for granted this world would always be there, regenerating itself and working in harmony. Most of us still hold dear these images of a world populated by elephants, dolphins, whales, and lions. It's an image that's upheld by Disney movies and the National Geographic channel, but it is no longer a reality.

Today most big animals live on industrial farms. They both outweigh and outnumber other lifeforms on our planet. Altogether, domesticated animals weigh around 700 million tons, while humans weigh 300 million tons, and large wild animals weigh less than 100 million tons.[27]

We have created a gross imbalance. A groundbreaking report by the Intergovernmental Science-Policy Platform on Biodiversity and Ecosystem Services (IPBES) found that one million species are in danger of extinction, and human activity is the cause.[28]

"The health of ecosystems on which we and all other species depend on is deteriorating more rapidly than ever. We are eroding the foundations of our economies, livelihoods, food security, health, and quality of life worldwide."
Sir Robert Watson, Chair of IPBES[29]

Some species threatened with extinction have not even been discovered yet. Between 1999 and 2015, over 2,000 new species were found in the Amazon. In 2014 and 2015, 216 previously unknown plants, 93 fish, 32 amphibians, 20 mammals, 19 reptiles and one bird were uncovered,[30] showing how much diversity we are destroying for the sake of the standard Western diet[31]. And, as we saw earlier, we are losing a football field's worth of uncharted, un-researched, undisturbed, pristine rainforest every second.

The vicious cycle is speeding up—we are playing with fire.

RESPECTING MOTHER EARTH
Is there something we can do?

Yes, there is. And there is still hope. If we can shift our diets, we can begin to turn things around. There is still a narrow window of time. And the time is now. A global food system based on a plant-based diet is a vital part of the remedy.

A new report by the international journal Science of the Total Environment explored over 300 different food system scenarios, all based around stopping deforestation. The standard Western diet[32] has the highest greenhouse gas emissions out of any dietary choice. In contrast, organic, plant-based food systems had negative greenhouse gas emissions, because the extra vegetation helps absorb carbon.[33]

Put simply, a meat-dominant diet releases unprecedented amounts of carbon into the atmosphere, whereas a plant-dominant diet absorbs that carbon out of the air. What's more, freeing up the land currently used for livestock would offer us opportunities to reforest and rewild areas that are currently barren, creating new habitats and breathing space for all species on earth. This space would drastically reduce the risk of future global pandemics (more on this in a moment). Finally, we would not have the millions of tons of toxic animal waste to dispose of, nor billions of animals to water, which would enable us to clean up our oceans and conserve freshwater supplies.

The result of a global shift towards plant-based living: a greener planet, one that we can pass on to future generations without shame or guilt.

At the current rate, animal agriculture will gobble up and pollute the world's land and freshwater reserves within thirty years. Within the next thirty years, the planet will be home to an extra two billion people. The diet we choose in the coming years will have a huge impact on the planet. The science is in and it's sobering. We need to urgently reassess our lifestyles and diets, as it is clear that any diet centered around meat and dairy will take a greater toll on the world's resources than a diet focused around vegetables, pulses, grains, nuts and seeds.[34]

I know that climate change is a complex and divisive topic. And I am not trying to suggest that animal agriculture is the only cause. Going more plant-based is not the only remedy required to solve all our ecological and climate problems, but no solution is complete without it.

There is no more time for indecision and hiding behind others. It is all of our collective and individual responsibility to protect and preserve our shared home.

Together, _REBEL VEGANS_ can save the planet.

6

HEALTH

PLANT-BASED POWER

"Let food be thy medicine, and medicine be thy food."
Hippocrates, the father of medicine[1]

For over a hundred years, meat and dairy have been held up as pinnacles of a healthy diet. This century of mass media marketing has made us believe that animal proteins are somehow integral to our survival, that it made us human and top of the food chain.

The truth is these foods threaten both our individual health and our global health. They give us cancer, heart disease, obesity and diabetes. Industrial farming creates the perfect conditions for antibiotic-resistant superbugs, not to mention zoonotic diseases such as MERS, SARS, vCJD (mad cow disease) and more recently, Covid.

Put succinctly, eating animals is slowly killing us.

GLOBAL HEALTH:
THE MEAT INDUSTRY AND GLOBAL PANDEMICS

ZOONOTIC DISEASES AND THE NEXT PANDEMIC

Pandemics are neither accidents nor coincidences. Sixty percent of all infectious diseases in humans[2] and 75% of all emerging infectious diseases are zoonotic.[3] Zoonotic means diseases that originate from animals, either wild or domesticated, and pass to humans.

Until recently, animals and humans lived more separately and had fewer interactions. There was a natural barrier between us, which to a certain degree protected us.[4] So-called disease reservoirs (also known as virus reservoirs, reservoirs of infection or natural reservoirs) were further away from us. A disease reservoir is the population of animals where an infectious pathogen (such as a virus) naturally lives and reproduces.[5]

The way we produce our food has eroded that barrier, and as a result, we are in closer proximity to pathogens, and at higher risk of virus epidemics.

According to the United Nations Environment Program (UNEP), a new infectious disease emerges in humans every four months.[6] While many of these diseases originate in wildlife (in so-called virus reservoirs), the bridge between wild animals and humans is livestock, and in particular intensively reared livestock.

Why?

It makes more sense when you consider that farm animals are bred to be almost identical—there is no genetic diversity to provide resilience or resistance to infection. After all, livestock are grown for production characteristics (like being heavier than their normal counterparts), rather than for immune strength. What's more, these animals are kept in crowded, unsanitary, unnatural conditions that make it impossible for them to be healthy—indeed they are kept alive with drugs.

Zoonotic viruses are opportunistic. They tend to affect hosts already stressed by environmental conditions. The 70 billion factory-farmed animals in the food system today fit that bill perfectly. These vulnerable animals are a Petri dish for infections and live in close proximity to humans.

Our food systems are a disaster waiting to happen.

Zoonotic viruses are not new. Some scientists hypothesize that flu first became a human disease when the Chinese domesticated ducks around 4,000 years ago, and brought that animal disease reservoir into human communities for the first time.[7] Humans can also catch flu from pigs and horses.[8] The H1N1 influenza virus caused the 1918 Spanish flu, thought to have originated from a midwestern pig farm[9], and the mad cow disease epidemic that hit the United Kingdom in the early 1990s[10] was caused by feeding bone meal to herbivores—something that, worryingly, is still happening today.

Scientists have been warning for decades that global pandemics are a serious threat. And yet little has been done to prevent them from occurring.[11]

In the last few years, several zoonotic diseases have made the headlines, but they have all felt remote. SARS in 2003 remained in Asia, MERS in 2012 stayed in the Middle East. Ebola in 2014 was centered in Africa. It was easy for the West to largely ignore these epidemics, to attribute them to different conditions in faraway cultures. We don't ride camels, eat monkeys or handle bats in wet markets. Our meat comes plastic-wrapped, sanitized and safe. This had nothing to do with us. This could not happen to us. We were wrong.

Ignoring inconvenient science seems to be a running theme in this story. We have known for a while that the way we eat poses a dire threat to global health, but we have looked the other way and failed to address it.

After the SARS outbreak in 2003, an essay in the American Journal of Public Health accepted that "changing the way humans treat animals—most basically, ceasing to eat them or, at the very least, radically limiting the quantity of them eaten—is largely off the radar as a significant preventative measure."[12]

In other words, one of the most effective ways we could reduce the risk of future pandemics was basically ignored by governments and global health authorities. Instead of listening to science, they refused to challenge the status quo, and accepted defeat.

To say that zoonotic viruses are just about wet markets and wild meat is to ignore a huge part of the equation. With the emergence of Covid-19, many have been quick to blame the Wuhan wet market and the trade of wild animals. Health authorities, including the head of the World Health Organization, have called for a clampdown on the sale of exotic animal meat, while remaining silent on the role of conventional food production.

The truth is that zoonotic viruses are an expanding threat, because we are increasingly encroaching on natural ecosystems, which serve as virus reservoirs. Prior to the industrial revolution, our contact with wild animals was limited, our settlements and agricultural endeavors were relatively small. These days, it's a whole other story, as we saw in the environment section.

We have taken once pristine land and transformed it, we have razed ecosystems to the ground to exploit them for crops, resource extraction, human settlements, but mostly for animal agriculture. This has provided pathogens with opportunities to spill over from wild animals to humans, often via farm animals.

At the same time, our conventional, large-scale, industrial farming practices have pushed small farmers into closer contact with wild animals. When large livestock firms lost market share in China, the government encouraged smallholders to breed and sell wild game. When local fishers in West Africa were pushed out of coastal waters by foreign trawlers in the 1970s, reliance on bush meat skyrocketed, leading to outbreaks of HIV and Ebola.

It is easy to point the finger at other people's taste for strange delicacies, while ignoring the West's reliance on pork, beef and chicken. There is a bigger issue at play here. Yes, contact with wild animals increases the risk of zoonotic diseases, but our industrial farming practices offer the perfect conditions for these viruses to spread. As these conditions increasingly intensify and multiply, we must now place responsibility where it ought to be—on the global, profit-driven, meat-centered food system.[13]

We have been lucky this time. I know it doesn't feel like it. At the time of writing, Covid has killed 4 million people worldwide.[14] But what would that number be if it was a more virulent and lethal virus?

Death Rate % vs Disease

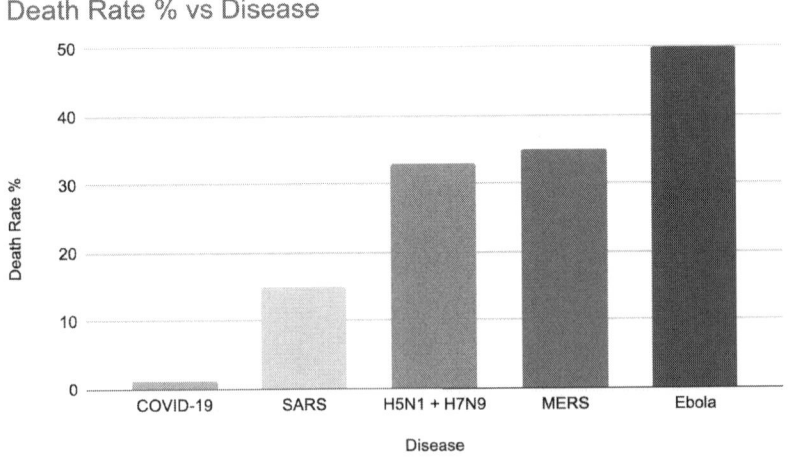

SARS has a death rate of 15%[15], MERS has a death rate of 35%[16], while Ebola has a death rate of 50%.[17] Other recent viruses, such as the H5N1 and H7N9 avian flus that originated in Chinese poultry farms, killed over a third of people infected.[18] HIV was a death sentence for 15 years until a drug treatment was found. Covid-19 has a death rate of 1.4%.[19] Almost everyone survives it.

So, while it might not feel like a blessing, Mother Nature has been pretty kind to us on this occasion. We have been given an opportunity and life-saving lesson if we are humble enough to listen and learn. Covid-19 has shown us that a pandemic can very quickly become global, and that our food systems are in large part to blame. But it also demonstrated we can adapt and change our behaviors when faced with a global emergency.

The question is not whether we will have another pandemic, but when. If we continue to consume animals, it is only a matter of time before it happens again, and there's a strong risk the next virus will be more virulent, more lethal and more transmissible. What's more, we may not have any tools left to combat a pandemic.

Why? Because there is more to the problem than simply encroaching on natural ecosystems and closing the gap between virus reservoirs and humans. The drugs and methods used on industrial animal farms are also part of the problem.

ANTIBIOTIC RESISTANCE
Not only are these pandemics and zoonotic threats multiplying, but controlling them is becoming more complicated. Antibiotics are no longer as effective as they once were. The invention of penicillin (the first modern antibiotic) in 1928 changed world history, and provided us with the ability to prevent bacterial infections. But the effectiveness and easy access to antibiotics has led to their overuse, and as a result, some bacteria have built up resistance.

In its Antimicrobial Resistance Global Report, the World Health Organization states that antimicrobial resistance is a widespread "serious threat [that] is no longer a prediction for the future, it is happening right now in every region of the world and has the potential to affect anyone, of any age, in any country."[20]

Antibiotics have been over-used and exploited, mostly by commercial livestock farmers, both to prevent the spread of disease in dirty, overcrowded feedlots, and to increase animal size, meat production and profits.

Although the FDA banned using medically important antibiotics as growth promoters in 2017[21], the quantity of antibiotics sold for food-producing animals has increased.[22] In 2020, 160,000 tons of antibiotics were fed to farm animals. If the current trends continue, this number will grow to 200,000 tons by 2030.[23] In many countries, 80% of the total consumption of antibiotics is in the animal sector.[24] Consequently, we are seeing the rise of antibiotic-resistant superbugs.

Another vicious cycle has developed where our current food system creates the perfect conditions to support viruses that are putting us all under threat, while also weakening the tools we have to prevent pandemics and fight infectious disease.

It is a disaster waiting to happen.

Or rather, it is already happening. Some antibiotics given to farm animals, including penicillin and tetracycline, are the same as the ones used to treat humans. People who eat meat, dairy and poultry are exposed to both antibiotic-resistant bacteria and low doses of antibiotic residues in these animal products, which results in the drugs not working as effectively.[25] The CDC's report on Antibiotic Resistance Threats in the United States, published in 2019, revealed that more than 2.8 million antibiotic resistant infections happen every year in the US, and more than 35,000 people die as a result.[26]

> *"A lack of effective antibiotics is as serious a security threat as a sudden and deadly disease outbreak. Strong, sustained action across all sectors is vital if we are to turn back the tide of antimicrobial resistance and keep the world safe."*
> **Dr. Tedros Adhanom Ghebreyesus,**
> **Director-General of WHO, 2017[27]**

The Covid-19 pandemic has shone a light on our global food systems—its dangers, failings and blind spots. This offers us a once-in-a-lifetime opportunity. Meat is kept artificially cheap, but how cheap is it if it causes millions of deaths and global lockdowns, as Covid is doing? We are being called to question our lifestyle choices and move towards a global food system that stops the spread of zoonotic diseases. One based on plants rather than animals.

Interestingly, a shift away from meat and towards plants is also an absolute must when it comes to our individual health.

> *"The world is heading towards a post-antibiotic era, in which many common infections will no longer have a cure and, once again, kill unabated. No action today means no cure tomorrow. At a time of multiple calamities in the world, we cannot allow the loss of essential medicines—essential cures for many millions of people—to become the next global crisis."*
> **Dr Margarat Chan, Director-General WHO[28]**

ZOONTOIC DISEASE[29]

A zoonotic disease (also known as zoonosis) is a disease caused by an infectious agent (such as bacteria, fungi, virus or parasite) that has jumped from an animal to a human.

Examples of zoonotic diseases:

- Anthrax (grazing herbivores like cattle, sheep, goats, horses, camels and pigs)
- Bird flu (wild birds and domesticated birds like chickens)
- Bovine spongiform encephalopathy or mad cow disease, BSE (cattle)
- Covid-19 (suspected: bats, felines, raccoon dogs, minks)
- Cysticercosis (pigs and cattle)
- Ebola virus (monkeys, fruit bats, gorillas, chimpanzees)
- HIB (non-human primates)
- Leprosy (armadillos, monkeys, rabbits, mice)
- Lyme disease (deer, wolves, birds, dogs, rodents, rabbits)
- Q fever (livestock and other domestic animals)
- Rabies (dogs, bats, monkeys, raccoons, foxes, cattle, goats, sheep, horses, mongooses)
- Rift valley fever (livestock, buffaloes, camels)
- SARS (bats, civets)
- Smallpox (monkeys or horses)
- Swine influenza (pigs)
- Toxoplasmosis (cats, livestock, poultry)

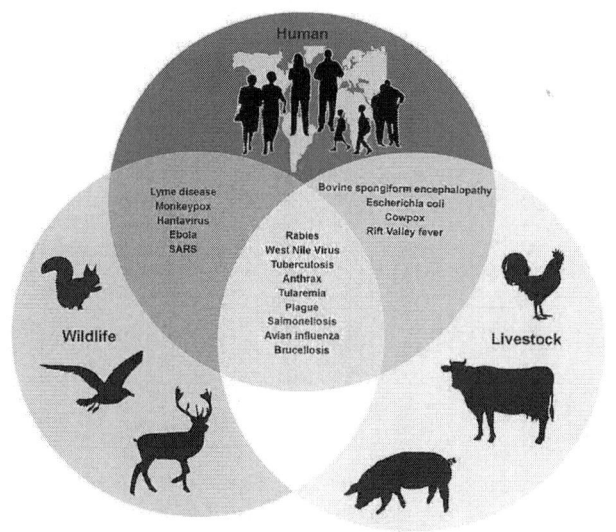

Image source:[30]

INDIVIDUAL HEALTH:

*"So I am living without fats, without meat, without fish,
but am feeling quite well this way. It always seems to me
that man was not born to be a carnivore."*
Albert Einstein in 1954 at age 75.[31]

THE MEAT INDUSTRY AND CHRONIC DISEASE

Even if we put to one side the ominous clouds of pandemics and superbugs, we cannot escape the tangible reality that animal products are undeniably not good for us. Eating meat is associated with a higher risk of non-communicable diseases, like cancer, heart disease, diabetes, obesity and Alzheimer's. While these are experienced individually, these are also, in a sense, global epidemics caused by our meat-centric diets.

Diet and disease are directly linked. I always say that every time you eat, you are either feeding disease or fighting it. It may be cliché to say "food is medicine," but it is also a truism and they are words to live by. Food can also be your poison. The key to your health and longevity is at the end of your fork! It's an incredibly powerful realization when you discover you hold the keys to improve your health and live longer.

In this section, I want to briefly demonstrate how meat, fish and dairy impact our health. We have been fed a lie, that animal products are necessary for our wellbeing.

If we are serious about living a healthy life, then we need to debunk the lies, expose the marketing misinformation, and open up to the latest findings.

As we stumble out of lockdowns, this is our opportunity to rethink and create our best lives.

CHRONIC INFLAMMATION - THE ROOT OF THE ISSUE

To understand the impact of the standard Western diet[32] on health, it is important to understand the process of inflammation in the body.

There are two types of inflammation: acute and chronic. One is beneficial and helps the body heal. The other sets the scene for chronic disease.

Acute inflammation is short-lived and part of the body's tools for healing. It is designed to help you recover from injury or illness, by neutralizing a virus or reducing the movement in a sprained ankle. If you injure yourself or come into contact with toxins, your immune system jumps into action and releases cytokines (these are immune molecules that pass messages between cells) and white blood cells to deal with the issue. Once the problem has been dealt with, your immune system switches off its defenses, and the symptoms of acute inflammation disappear. The swelling subsides and all is well.

Chronic inflammation is acute inflammation that does not go away. Your immune system automatically launches an inflammatory response when it is faced with a threat. In other words, when it is faced with something that should not be in your body. It is supposed to flare up, deal with the problem, and go away. But when you are constantly exposed to toxins and pathogens, your immune system is on constant high alert.

The result is chronic inflammation. Your body's inflammatory response does not switch off and can begin to damage healthy cells, tissues and organs. Over time, this leads to DNA damage, cellular dysfunction and internal scarring. And this in turn leads to the development of several chronic diseases.

Chronic inflammation makes it harder for your immune system to do its job. It is a symptom of an immune system that no longer knows what to respond to. Think of your immune system as your body's special forces team. This team patrols your body, identifying threats and dealing with them. When chronic inflammation is present, these special forces never have a moment to switch off. Therefore, they are not as effective and eventually begin making mistakes that damage the body and make it more prone to disease.

Researchers from the National Institute of Health found that worldwide, three out of every five people die of diseases caused by chronic inflammation. These include cardiovascular disease, stroke, chronic respiratory disease, cancer, obesity and diabetes.[33] Chronic inflammation also makes it harder for your body to fight a virus.

It is not a coincidence that people already struggling with chronic inflammation or related diseases are more prone to getting Covid or dying of it. When it comes to keeping your immune system strong, avoiding foods that cause chronic inflammation is key.

Certain foods cause a temporary (or acute) inflammatory response. When these foods are eaten regularly, this temporary inflammation can become chronic. The standard Western diet[34] is to blame—high in inflammatory processed foods and low in anti-inflammatory whole foods.

Basically, we are eating foods laden with chemicals and not eating enough foods that contain immune-supporting nutrients. Meat and dairy play a big part here, because they contain residues of animal medicines and are known to trigger an immune response.

Another way eating meat increases the likelihood of chronic inflammation is that it impacts the composition of the gut's microbiome, which in turn affects how the immune system works. A high intake of red and processed meat can decrease the digestive system's mucosal layer, making it more permeable to bacteria and pathogens. The immune system reacts to these pathogens by launching an inflammatory response.[35]

When it comes to dairy, the problem lies in what else is present in milk. As mentioned earlier, dairy cows are made to provide twice the amount of milk they would naturally produce. Because of this, they contract something called mastitis. Mastitis is a painful inflammatory condition that affects the mammary glands. Healthy milk from healthy cows contains under 100,000 somatic cells per milliliter. Somatic cells are white blood cells, in other words: pus. A count of 200,000 somatic cells per milliliter indicates there is an infection.

The industry is legally allowed to sell milk that contains 750,000 somatic cells per milliliter.[36] Not only is this a gross admission that dairy cows are sick, it also means the milk you buy from the supermarket is likely to make you sick too. The immune system responds to these somatic cells in the same way as it would an invader, by increasing levels of inflammation.

I'm not saying meat and dairy are the only cause of chronic inflammation and illness. High sugar foods, artificial trans-fats from hydrogenated oils, refined carbohydrates, pesticide residues, pollutants, stress, smoking and excess alcohol can also trigger and maintain chronic inflammation. However, meat and dairy are a big part of the Western diet,[37] and studies show that people who eat this type of diet have a higher risk of chronic disease.

The problem is on our plate and so is the answer.

Plant-based diets help lower inflammation levels thanks to the antioxidants found in fruits and vegetables. A whole food plant-based diet contains sixty-four times more inflammation-busting antioxidants compared to the standard American diet.[38]

OBESITY

Obesity is defined as excessive body fat that causes a health risk. A body mass index (BMI) of over 25 is considered overweight, a BMI of over 30 is considered obese.

High BMI and elevated fasting blood sugar are the two most important health risk factors in the United States. Put simply, the number one cause of death in the USA is the Western diet.[39]

We have become our own worst enemies and our own biggest threat. Today more people die of excess sugar consumption than they do from war or terrorism. More people will die from over consumption than starvation. And the meat industry is involved in both extremes.

"For the first time in history, you are your worst enemies. Fewer people died in 2017 due to UN violence than due to obesity, car accidents and suicides.

Statistically, you have a greater chance of killing yourself than any soldier or terrorist. Sugar is a greater danger than gunpowder. You are more likely to die of drinking too much cola than being blown up by Al-Qaeda."
Yuval Noah Harari, Author of Sapiens[40]

Obesity rates have tripled since 1975. The latest statistics from the World Health Organization show that almost two billion adults worldwide are overweight or obese.[41] In the United States, obesity rates went from 30.1% in 1999 to 42.4% in 2017.[42]

Chronic inflammation and obesity go hand in hand. That's because the accumulation of excessive fat stimulates the release of inflammatory chemicals, which predispose the body to be in a pro-inflammatory state. What's more, high levels of body fat reduce the production of adiponectin, a hormone that helps regulate glucose levels and break down fatty acids, thereby making obesity harder to overcome.[43]

Interestingly, meat-centric diets have also been touted as an answer to the obesity crisis. We had the Atkins' diet in the 90s, and the modern version, the keto diet. Centered around eating animal proteins and avoiding carbohydrates, this regime has grown in popularity in recent years. Yes, it can lead to temporary weight loss. But not as much long-term weight loss as going vegan.

In January 2021, the journal Nature Medicine published a study that compared the effects of an animal-based ketogenic diet versus a plant-based diet. The results were clear. Participants who ate a carbohydrate-rich, plant-based diet ate more food, but lost body fat and retained muscle. While those who followed a keto diet ate less food, but retained fat while losing muscle. The researchers attributed these results to the fact that plant foods contain more fiber.[44]

DIABETES

Diabetes is another worldwide epidemic. In 2019, 473 million adults worldwide were diabetic[45,] and this disease caused an estimated 1.5 million deaths.[46]

Diabetes is a condition where the pancreas does not produce enough insulin (a hormone that regulates blood sugar) or where the body cannot use the insulin effectively. As a result, blood sugar levels keep rising, and this leads to serious damage to many of the body's systems, particularly nerves and blood vessels. Being diabetic also increases the risk of heart attacks and strokes.[47]

You might be wondering what diabetes, a disease centered around blood sugar, has to do with meat. According to a review of studies published in The American Journal of Clinical Nutrition, eating red meat increases the risk of diabetes. Just one 3.5 ounces (99 gram) serving of meat increases a person's risk of type 2 diabetes by 19%.[48] One of the reasons for this is meat's high content of heme-iron.[49]

Diabetes also increases levels of chronic inflammation. High levels of glucose in the blood cause the formation of advanced glycation agents, which initiate oxidative stress—a condition where there are more free radicals in the body than there are antioxidant defenses.

In other words, there are more damaging molecules circulating in your body than there are molecules that can defend your body against the damage. This causes a further increase in inflammation that makes it harder for your cells to respond to insulin. It's a vicious cycle.

The solution for more and more diabetics is to switch to a plant-based diet, one that includes plenty of vegetables, plant proteins like beans, nuts, seeds, whole grains and fruit. A 74-week study, published in the American Journal of Clinical Nutrition, found that a plant-based diet controlled blood sugar three times more effectively than a traditional diabetes diet that limited calories and carbohydrates.[50] The reason for this is that plants contain plenty of fiber, which adds bulk to meals without increasing blood sugar levels, helps keep you fuller for longer, and provides nutrients for healthy gut flora.

Even more exciting, scientists have found that a vegan diet can reverse diabetes. In another study, diabetes patients following a personalized whole food plant-based diet protocol were able to come off medication after 20 weeks.[51]

CARDIOVASCULAR DISEASE AND CHOLESTEROL

Cardiovascular disease is an umbrella term that covers disorders of the heart and blood vessels—high blood pressure (hypertension), heart attacks (coronary heart disease), and strokes (cerebrovascular disease). Cholesterol is the risk factor in all these disorders because it causes plaque deposits that narrow blood vessels, while also increasing levels of inflammation.

A study published by the United States' National Institutes of Health found that eating meat triples the amount of the chemicals related to heart disease. Gut bacteria from something called trimethylamine N-oxide (TMAO) as a byproduct of digesting meat. Research shows that TMAO enhances the formation of cholesterol deposits on blood vessel walls. It also impedes normal clotting responses, increasing the risk of heart attacks and strokes.

But the study also found that levels of TMAO were reversible. When participants switched to plant proteins for a month, their TMAO levels decreased significantly.[52]

Cardiovascular disease is a lifestyle disease. It is caused by an excessive intake of saturated fat and cholesterol. These fatty substances build up in blood vessels as plaque, impeding blood flow. The biggest sources of saturated fat and cholesterol in the Western diet[53] are dairy and meat. Incidentally, plant-based diets are very low in saturated fat and dietary cholesterol. It is incredible to think that even though this is accepted scientifically and common knowledge in the medical community, the United States dietary guidelines continue to promote meat products and a daily intake of three cups of dairy.

A review published in the Journal of the American Medical Association analyzed six studies and found that for every 0.01 ounces (300 milligrams) of dietary cholesterol consumed per day, the risk of cardiovascular disease increased by 17%, while the risk of all-cause mortality increased by 18%.[54]

To give you an idea of what that means in terms of food, an egg contains around 0.007 ounces (212 milligrams) of cholesterol, 3.5 ounces (99 grams) of shrimp contains 0.0068 ounces (194 milligrams) of cholesterol, and 3.5 ounces (99 grams) of ground beef contains around 0.003 ounces (90 milligrams) of cholesterol.[55]

Heart disease is the top cause of death globally. In the United States, a person dies of cardiovascular disease every thirty-six seconds. Heart disease causes one in every four deaths.[56] And it is an absolutely preventable illness.

If we made healthier lifestyle choices, we could prevent most cases. In 2017, researchers reviewed forty-nine studies comparing plant-based diets with omnivorous diets. Their findings? Plant-based diets lowered total cholesterol levels by 15-30%.[57]

A study published by the Journal of the American Heart Association followed over 12,000 adults for a period of twenty-five years and analyzed their dietary data. It found that the more plant foods were consumed and the fewer animal products were consumed, the lower the risk of cardiovascular disease. In fact, plant-based diets reduced the risk of heart disease by 16% and the risk of cardiovascular death by 32%.[58] The same study found something else that is relevant here—eating fish and low-fat dairy (both generally considered to be superfoods and essential for good health) did not provide any benefits for cardiovascular health.

We have the solution at our fingertips, and we've known about it for years. We need to harness the healing power of plants.

CANCER

There is no easy way to talk about Cancer. I feel like it haunts most of our families in the developed nations. This is an epidemic that has touched all of our lives. Worldwide, an estimated 19.3 million new cancer cases, and almost 10 million cancer deaths happened in 2020. The global cancer burden is expected to almost double to 28.4 million by 2040.[59]

I remember when the World Health Organization ruffled feathers in 2015 when they published their Meat and Cancer report. The report examined over 800 peer-reviewed studies and found a correlation between the consumption of red meat (beef, pork, veal, lamb, mutton, horse, goat) and processed meat (all meats that have been transformed through salting, curing, fermenting, smoking, and other processes to enhance flavor and shelf life, such as hot dogs, sausages, corned beef, beef jerky, canned meat, and meat sauces) and the incidence of colorectal cancers.

On the strength of the data, the International Agency for Research on Cancer classified red meat as a Group 2A Carcinogen (probably carcinogenic to humans) and processed meat as a Group 1A Carcinogen (carcinogenic to humans).[60] To put this into perspective, tobacco is a Group 1A carcinogen, and nobody is in doubt of its effects.

The report found that every 1.7 ounces (50 gram) portion of processed meat increases the risk of colorectal cancer by 18% and that every 3.5 ounces (100 gram) portion of red meat increases the risk of colorectal cancer by 17%.[61]

Though groundbreaking, this report caused a quick uproar before being relegated to the mountain of information governments choose to ignore when it comes to their health policies and nutritional guidelines.

While the WHO's report could show a correlation between meat-eating and cancer, it fell short of demonstrating causation—the way meat causes cells to mutate remained unclear. However, this has changed in June 2021.

A new study published in the journal Cancer Discovery has identified specific patterns of DNA damage triggered by meat-centric diets. This damage, called alkylation, was significantly associated with processed and unprocessed red meat. The specific compounds involved are nitroso compounds (which are made from heme-iron and are plentiful in red meat), and nitrates (often found in processed meat). Patients with the highest levels of alkylation damage had a 47% greater risk of colorectal cancer deaths, compared with patients with lower levels of damage.[62]

Another link between meat and cancer was explained in a study by the Proceedings of the National Academy of Sciences of the United States of America. Researchers discovered that the human immune system attacks a sugar in red meat called Neu5Gc, causing chronic inflammation that can eventually trigger cancer. According to the lead author of the study, "red meat is great, if you want to live to 45."[63]

There's more. A new study of over 300,000 women found that a diet high in meat, dairy and processed sugar increases the risk of breast cancer by 12%. The research, carried out by the World Health Organization, the Imperial College in London, and the Catalan Institute of Oncology, concluded that the reason for the spike in cancer risk was these foods' inflammatory properties.[64]

Again, the answer is all around us and always has been—a plant-based diet.

A review of studies published in the journal Clinical Reviews in Food and Nutrition found that a vegan diet can reduce the risk of cancer by at least 15%. The researchers concluded that the benefits are due to the fact that plant foods are high in fiber, antioxidants, and vitamins that support the immune system and protect against cell mutations.[65]

Another study, this time published in the Journal of Unexplored Medical Data, found that a plant-based diet can protect against the fifteen leading causes of death, including many cancers and chronic diseases, such as diabetes, heart disease and obesity.[66] It goes on to conclude that adopting a vegan diet centered around whole, natural foods is "a simple and cost-effective intervention that can be used alone to prevent disease or adjunct with conventional treatment when the disease is already present."

Profoundly simple and life-changing knowledge. All we need to do is start putting it into practice.

DEMENTIA AND ALZHEIMER'S

Our cognitive health is a choice we make with every bite we take.

Research shows that the saturated fats found in meat, dairy, processed foods, and fast foods increases the risk of cognitive decline. This is because these foods increase chronic inflammation, and inflammation causes the build-up of plaques that lead to cognitive impairment.

Today, there are over 40 million people suffering from Alzheimer's, a condition characterized by amyloid plaques in the brain that impact mood, memory, and motor skills. People with Alzheimer's struggle to reason, and experience personality changes, a gradual decline in memory, and problems speaking and moving.

By 2050, it is estimated Alzheimer's will affect 150 million people. That means that as many of you, my readers, get older, you will likely either suffer from it or know a friend or loved one who has it. If you live to 85 or older, your chances of getting it are one in two.[67]

Pretty grim stuff. But there is increasing and exciting evidence showing that dementia is not an inevitable part of getting older. It can be prevented with the right lifestyle choices, particularly what we choose to put on our plate.

A study published in the journal Innovation in Ageing examined the association between a plant-based diet and dementia risk in over 12,000 people. It found that vegetarians had a lower risk of dementia compared to people eating an omnivorous diet.[68] That's because a plant-based diet, rich in antioxidants and healthy fats, helps protect brain health. In fact, research shows that a diet based around plants can reduce the risk of Alzheimer's by more than 50%.[69]

In parts of the world where people eat a predominantly plant-based diet, for example, the Greek island of Ikaria (one of the world's Blue Zones, renowned for its inhabitants commonly reaching their 100th birthday), people live on average eight to ten years longer than Americans with almost no cases of dementia. In Ikaria, you have less than a 10% chance of getting Alzheimer's.[70]

BUT FISH IS HEALTHY, ISN'T IT?

Many people stop eating meat, but keep eating fish, believing it is one of the healthiest sources of protein and brain-friendly fats. We need essential fatty acids for our brain, as well as our cell membranes and nervous system. They are also important for regulating blood pressure, the immune system and inflammation. They're called "essential" because the body does not make them itself, and we must obtain them from food.

There are three Omega-3 fatty acids: alpha-linolenic acid (ALA), which is found in plants such as flaxseed, which the body converts into eicosapentaenoic acid (EPA) and docosahexaenoic (DHA). Fish obtain their ALA Omega-3 from algae and then convert it to EPA and DHA. This conversion can be difficult for the human body, which is why some people insist that oily fish is essential to obtain enough Omega-3. But this is incorrect.

Research from Cochrane finds that EPA and DHA from oily fish or fish oil supplements have little or no effect on heart health.[71] ALA from plant foods, on the other hand, did slightly reduce the risk of cardiovascular illness. A review of studies published in the British Journal of Nutrition found that ALA from plant foods helps reduce the risk of heart disease.[72] In other words, plant-based Omega-3 is better for you. Just like protein, it is more efficient to get Omega-3 straight from the source (plants) instead of the middle man (animals).

As we learn more about fish and fish oils, things go from bad to worse. It turns out they could do more harm than good.

The first issue comes from methyl-mercury, an environmental pollutant found in fish. A study in Eastern Finland found that men who ate the most fish had the highest levels of mercury, and an increased risk of cardiovascular death.[73]

Our oceans are polluted, not just by mercury, but also by polychlorinated biphenyls and dioxins, which are known neurotoxins. These pollutants accumulate in fish, and this cancels out any potential benefits from their Omega-3.

Pollutants aside, shellfish like mussels and oysters accumulate bacteria and viruses from their environment. One of these viruses is norovirus, which is one of the most common causes of food poisoning. Another is hepatitis E, which spreads via a fecal-oral route. Livestock, such as pigs, can act as reservoirs of hepatitis E. High levels of the virus have been detected in wastewater and manure from industrial pig farms. Animal waste enters waterways, it can then accumulate in shellfish, and end up on your plate.

Farmed fish is no better. The farms are overcrowded, the fish are stressed, unhealthy, and pumped with antibiotics, anti-parasite treatments, disinfectants, and feed additives. What's more, farmed fish usually contain less Omega-3 because they are fed a diet rich in Omega-6, as well as fishmeal and fish oils. You read that right—wild fish are caught to feed farmed fish (and livestock). Almost 90% of some species of fish have been depleted, all this because of the myth of brain-healthy fish.[74]

The solution? Eating plant foods that are naturally rich in ALA Omega-3, such as walnuts, flaxseeds and chia seeds, or taking an algal-based vegan Omega-3 supplement that provides EPA and DHA without the pollutants or viruses.

BUT DAIRY IS HEALTHY, ISN'T IT?

In a word, no. Let me tell you why.

Dairy products are one of the top sources of saturated fat and cholesterol-raising fat in the American diet.[75]

Dairy contains IGF-1 (insulin-like growth factor 1), which has been associated with an increased risk of cancer, diabetes, and chronic inflammation.[76]

Dairy can increase the risk of breast cancer by up to 80%.[77]
Dairy can increase the risk of prostate cancer by up to 65%.[78]

"Cows' milk protein may be the single most significant chemical carcinogen to which humans are exposed."
T Colin Campbell,
Professor of Nutritional Biochemistry at Cornell University[79]

We are told dairy is a superfood, that we need it for our bones, that it "does the body good". But the truth is it makes us sick. A recent study by the International Journal of Epidemiology studied 53,000 women over eight years and found that those who drank 2-3 glasses of milk (the current USDA recommended amount) had a 70-80% increased risk of breast cancer. Women who replaced cow's milk with soy milk were 32% less likely to have breast cancer.[80] Another study involving over 1 million participants noted that a high intake of dairy products was associated with a 65% increased risk of prostate cancer. Men following a plant-based diet had a 36% lower risk.[81]

Milk is good for your bones. I heard my mother say it a hundred times. Now my sisters are feeding their daughters cow's milk. In North America, we drink large glasses of milk every day under the assumption that it will keep our bones strong. But here's an interesting question—why do women who drink milk have a higher risk of brittle bones?

American women are the biggest consumers of dairy, and yet they have one of the highest rates of osteoporosis in the world. A study by the US National Dairy Council compared postmenopausal women who drank three 8 ounces (240 milliliters) glasses of skimmed milk a day for two years with women who drank no milk. The women who drank dairy lost bone at twice the rate of women who didn't.[82]

We need calcium. But we do not need dairy. There is nothing in dairy that we cannot get from plants. You can get calcium from leafy greens (like Swiss chard, broccoli and kale), as well as winter squash, almonds, and tofu. Calcium in certain plant foods is more bio-available than calcium in dairy.

According to the Harvard School of Public Health, dairy products have a calcium bioavailability of around 30%. This means that if a cup of milk contains 300 milligrams of calcium, the body will only absorb around 100 milligrams of calcium. On the other hand, calcium from bok choi (a leafy green similar to Swiss chard) has a bioavailability of 50%.

One cup of bok choi contains 160 milligrams of calcium, or 80 milligrams of bioavailable calcium, which makes a cup of bok choi comparable to a cup of milk in terms of calcium content. However, leafy greens also contain fiber and antioxidants that support health, whereas a cup of milk contains saturated fat that promotes disease.[83]

THE BLUE ZONES: ANOTHER WAY IS POSSIBLE

The Blue Zones are five remote regions in Europe, Latin America, Asia, and the United States, which stand out for having the highest number of centenarians in the world. While each region has its own unique diet, they have one thing in common—they're very light on meat and heavy on plants.

Dan Buettner, explorer and founder of the Blue Zones, examined and inventoried each region's diets to identify the pillars of their longevity. He found that their diet consists almost entirely of minimally processed plant food, foods like whole grains, greens, nuts, tubers and beans. People there eat meat on average five times a month.

What that means in practice is that one meal every week contains meat—everything else is plant-based. They drink mostly water, herbal tea, coffee, and some wine. They drink little or no cow's milk, and fizzy drinks hardly ever feature. As a result, inhabitants of the Blue Zones live longer, healthier, happier lives than people living elsewhere.

Unfortunately, as globalization spreads, even these areas are falling prey to the scourge of the Western diet.[84] Now, the gap between life spans in the Blue Zones and the rest of the world is gradually closing.[85] The arrival of processed foods, animal products and fast foods has pushed up the rate of chronic disease, even in the Blue Zones.[86] While this is bad news, it does at least show us the link between meat and disease and offers us a clear path towards a healthier way of life.

"And there you have it: The vast majority of the calories eaten in the traditional diets in the blue zones come from plant-based whole foods. Grains, greens, nuts, and beans are the four pillars of every longevity diet on Earth."
Dan Buettner, founder of the Blue Zones[87]

When it comes to driving forces for veganism, health is often at the forefront. It was for me. Covid has only placed a spotlight on a bigger problem that has so far remained hidden and rarely talked about. But it has highlighted something else—that when needed, the whole world can mobilize against a disease.

Something we do almost without thinking—eating meat—is leading to the health crises we face today. And the way we produce meat and dairy opens the door to pandemics like Covid. If we don't adapt, we will likely see further global pandemics. And next time we might end up with something more virulent and deadly.

The Western diet[88] is also in great part to blame for the obesity, cancer, and heart disease epidemics that kill millions of people every year. But both pandemics and chronic diseases are preventable: a plant-based diet is the solution we have been waiting for. By coming on this journey, you are part of the solution!

COMPARISON BETWEEN NON-COMMUNICABLE DISEASES (CAUSED BY WESTERN DIET), AND COVID.

Deaths from Covid 2019 to 2021: 3.98 million people.[89]

Deaths from noncommunicable diseases (lifestyle diseases): 41 million people each year. This equates to 71% of all deaths globally.

Top four causes of death:[90]

- **Cardiovascular disease:** 17.9 million deaths annually

- **Cancer:** 9.3 million deaths annually

- **Chronic respiratory diseases:** 4.1 million deaths annually

- **Diabetes:** 1.5 million deaths annually

"We have just been doing some calculations looking at the question of how much could we reduce mortality by shifting towards a healthy, more plant-based diet, not necessarily totally vegan, and our estimates are that about one-third of deaths could be prevented."
Dr Walter Willett,
Professor of epidemiology and nutrition
at Harvard Medical School, 2018[91]

7

SOCIAL STUDIES

THE IMPACT OF MEAT ON COMMUNITIES

"Injustice anywhere is a threat to justice everywhere."
Martin Luther King Jr

While researching this book while in isolation during the long lockdowns, several shocking reports came out exposing the terrible conditions of slaughterhouses in both the US and Europe. Finally we were seeing behind the tall walls of slaughterhouses and "meat packing" factories and I knew I had to investigate further and include it here as one of the driving forces that make veganism such an urgent and essential movement.

How our modern food system impacts society is an overlooked topic and is usually brushed under the carpet. It's not on any school syllabuses and the meat industry works hard to keep us in the dark.

It's time to bring these important civil liberties issues into the light. So, what does animal agriculture have to do with social issues?

A lot, as it happens.

I think it's important to go back to basics and debunk two myths surrounding industrial food production, and in particular the meat industry. The first is the theory that modern agriculture can feed the world. The second is that this industry creates good jobs and contributes to the economy. In reality, the meat industry contributes to world hunger, and the jobs it offers are on a par with modern slavery. And when it comes to Covid, it has willfully put both employees and consumers at risk.

Today's industrial meat industry doesn't just harm your personal health, animals, and the environment—it also causes huge suffering to humans within the system.

FEEDING FAMINE

If modern industrial food production can feed the world, why are people going hungry? Why is famine still happening?

Animal foods are not an energy-efficient way of eating. A report by Compassion in World Farming found that for every 100 calories of human-edible crops fed to livestock, we get only 17-30 calories of animal protein. It is not just a wasteful use of grain crops, but also the resources (land, water, energy) used to grow them.[1] For every 2 pounds (1 kilo) of animal protein, livestock is fed almost 12 pounds (6 kilos) of plant protein.

Famine is a growing problem. We find ourselves in the ridiculous situation where poorer developing countries need to export their harvests to rich countries instead of feeding their starving population. Many post-colonial or emerging nations need to grow these "cash crops" to pay off crippling debts at the expense of providing basic nourishment for the indigenous people.

We are part of this system that's taking the food out of their hands.

According to a recent analysis by the United Nations' World Food Program, 41 million people are currently teetering on the edge of famine, compared to 27 million people two years ago. This is not an unsolvable problem. A report by Cornell University found that the United States alone could feed 800 million people with grain that livestock eat.[2]

Clearly, the industrial animal industry is not feeding the world; quite the opposite in fact. But solutions are at our fingertips.

Industrial farms do not produce most of the world's food. There are more than 570 million farms in the world, and 90% of these are run by individuals or families. These small farms produce 80% of the world's food. According to the United Nations' FAO, investment in smallholder production is the most urgent and promising method for combating world hunger while minimizing the ecological impact of industrial agriculture.[3]

But even more relevant here is the fact that animal proteins are an inefficient use of resources; plants are fed to the animals instead of feeding people. The best way forward is directness. Let's cut out the middle-man and go straight to plant power!

DRIVING INEQUALITY

According to population forecasts, the world will be home to almost 10 billion people by 2050. Food production would have to increase by 50% to accommodate this. But, as we saw in the environment section, that would be a disaster for the planet. If food production increases along with the current trends, we would require a landmass twice the size of India. This would spell the end for many of the world's remaining forests and wild areas, releasing the carbon stored there, and accelerating climate collapse.

Climate change is a social issue as well as an ecological one. In 2020, 55 million people were forced to move from their countries because of extreme weather conditions.[4] The majority of these people find themselves in an even more precarious position. Uprooted from their home, they struggle to settle in countries where they are met with hostility and where they face financial hardship.

While climate change is now having an impact on developed countries, the countries that have so far fared the worst are low to middle-income countries. Natural disasters in Asia, Africa, Latin America and the Caribbean have cost over $108 billion in economic losses. The food production loss in these countries equates to 6.9 trillion calories per year (that's the annual calorie intake for 7 million adults).[5]

LOCAL SLAVERY: JOBS AND COMMUNITIES

According to an economic impact study commissioned by the North American Meat Institute, the meat and poultry industry creates 5.4 million jobs in the United States, with an estimated 527,019 jobs in production and packing, importing, sales, packaging and distribution.[6][7] But the kind of jobs we are talking about here are not jobs anyone would want, given the choice.

I've never heard anyone ever say that working in a meat-packing plant or slaughterhouse was their dream job. Who in their right mind would want to spend 10–12 hours a day killing animals, chopping carcasses, or cleaning blood, guts and shit off the kill floor, for minimum wage. This kind of work attracts people who have little choice in the matter.

In the United States, it is estimated that almost 40% of factory farm workers are illegal immigrants. These workers are vulnerable to exploitation. They are more likely to accept low wages and hazardous working conditions, and they are less likely to unionize. The meat industry capitalizes on their situation to abuse their rights. Human Rights Watch describes slaughterhouse work in the United States as a human rights crime.[8]

According to the worker advocacy group Project Protect Food System Workers, many factory farm workers operate dangerous equipment without proper training, making them more vulnerable to injuries and deaths. Like the recent death of a dairy worker who drowned in a manure pit containing the waste of more than 3,000 animals, while operating a manure vacuum truck.[9] He is not the first to suffocate in a waste pit. Many workers who have entered waste pits or "lagoons" to perform maintenance tasks have been asphyxiated by the hydrogen sulfide gas emitted by liquid manure. Unconscious, they quickly drown. Often, these incidents involve more than one person as co-workers attempt to rescue one another.[10]

Factory farmworkers are exposed to hazardous materials, such as particulate matter (from dry fecal matter, feed, animal hair and skin cells, feathers, fungi, dry soil and bacterial endotoxins[11]), ammonia and hydrogen sulfide gases. These are bad enough individually, and when combined, they cause serious health complications. As a result of inhaling this cocktail of chemicals, workers suffer from chronic respiratory disorders, asthma, cardiovascular disorders and premature death.[12]

Nothing slows production. One poultry farmer working for Tyson Foods (the largest meat producer in the US) reported that it is not uncommon for slaughterhouse workers to urinate on the production line or defecate in their pants—they are expected to keep working.[13] This fact is also reported by Oxfam America. Workers are often required to wear diapers because they are not allowed breaks.[14]

Imagine having to hoist live birds and lock them into shackles on a fast-moving line that takes them to the electric stun bath and then the mechanical blade. Workers have to shackle 35 birds a minute. The birds fight back. Once locked in place, the birds empty their bowels. Despite protective coverings, feces from flapping birds get into the workers' eyes, nose, mouth, and ears.[15]

Imagine having to spend your working life among animals that it is your job to abuse—whether that's by debeaking, tail docking, castrating, pushing or prodding them towards the stun gun, or disembowelling them.

Slaughterhouse workers are seven times more likely to suffer repetitive strain injuries than people in other types of work. In the United States, an average of two amputations every week involves slaughterhouse workers. Every month at least one Tyson Foods employee loses a finger or a limb.[16]

For her book Slaughterhouse, Gail Eisnitz, chief investigator for the Humane Farming Association, interviewed slaughterhouse workers equivalent to over two million hours of experience. Without exception, they told her they had beaten, strangled, boiled or dismembered animals alive.

Because of the speed at which employees are required to work, pigs and cattle are routinely skinned while they are still conscious, kicking and shrieking. This isn't just cruel to the animals, but dangerous for the workers too. Cows weigh several thousand pounds and can kick out and debilitate anyone near them.[17]

Much of this is caused by the speed of the production line. Instead of slowing things down, the US government has given the go-ahead to new rules that eliminate production line speed limits at pig slaughterhouses. The USDA said maximum line speeds were an "unnecessary regulatory obstacle to industry innovation." It is unclear how this will help reduce the high number of injuries suffered by meat plant workers.[18] Clearly, what is being protected is profit, not people.

There is often a lot of kickback against factory farmworkers. Footage from undercover animal rights activists that show workers abusing animals makes people, understandably, angry. But these workers are victims of the industry as much as the animals are. They too are being exploited and abused by a system that puts profits over people, animals and the planet.

Working in the meat industry is fraught with physical dangers, but the damage goes deeper. It leads to psychological damage and crime. Several studies show that factory farm workers consistently experience lower physical and psychological wellbeing, as well as an increased risk of negative coping strategies, such as abusing drugs and alcohol.[19]

It isn't surprising.

These employees are hired to kill animals that are largely gentle creatures. Carrying out their job requires workers to disconnect from what they are doing and from the sentient being in front of them. This causes emotional dissonance and leads to domestic violence, social withdrawal, anxiety, drug abuse, and Perpetrator-Induced Traumatic Syndrome, a form of PTSD. This is reflected in crime statistics. A study by criminologist Amy Fitzgerald states that "slaughterhouse employment increases total arrest rates, arrests for violent crimes, arrests for rape, and arrests for other sex offenses in comparison with other industries."[20]

We are not predators.

We are not designed to kill.

Animal cruelty is an indicator of a deep mental disturbance.

Robert K. Ressler, who developed profiles of serial killers for the Federal Bureau of Investigation (FBI), states that "murderers very often start out by killing or torturing animals." Studies show that violent or aggressive criminals are more likely to have abused animals as children.

According to a police study in Australia, most sexual homicide offenders have a history of animal cruelty. The school shootings that have been happening more and more frequently in the United States have a common theme—in most cases, the violence started with cruelty to animals.[21]

We've seen how this impacts workers in this industry, but what about us? Doesn't eating meat require us to somehow accept the cruelty that goes on behind closed doors? By accepting these unspoken beliefs, what is that doing to our psyche? We too, like the kill-floor workers, have to switch off the part of our natural, caring, compassionate nature, in order to keep consuming meat and dairy.

IMPACT ON THE COMMUNITY

Living near a slaughterhouse or large factory farm is a nightmare. Here are just some of the problems that nearby communities must endure.

The first is air pollution. CAFOs release large amounts of particulates (especially in dry seasons or dry regions where manure turns to dust), ammonia, hydrogen sulfide, methane and nitrous oxide, among others. These chemicals cause respiratory conditions, some of them are neurotoxic. Hydrogen sulfide poisoning can cause irreversible brain damage.

What's more, studies have found high levels of antibiotics and antibiotic-resistant genes in air samples downwind from feedlots.[22] Huge amounts of animal waste are disposed of by either spraying onto fields or in the air. Facilities can do this without a permit despite the reality of leaks, spills, and runoff.[23]

The second issue is drinking water quality. Phosphorus and nitrogen can leach into drinking water reservoirs, causing a potentially fatal blood disorder called blue baby syndrome.[24] Aside from the serious health implications, just imagine the smell for a moment. Then imagine living beside it for a lifetime!

And thirdly, higher rates of crime. A large statistical analysis by the University of Windsor and Michigan State University found that counties where slaughterhouses are located have four times the national average of violent arrest, and significantly higher rates of alcoholism, domestic abuse, and suicide.[25]

In some states, CAFOs are located in poor and African American communities. For example, in North Carolina, there are seven times more swine CAFOs in areas with the highest percentage of non-Caucasian residents compared with areas with the lowest percentage of non-Caucasian residents. People in these communities cannot afford to move. The proximity of these CAFOs leads to social, economic and health burdens to already disadvantaged communities.[26]

COVID HOTSPOTS

Far from helping to fight the spread of Covid, the meat industry has been capitalizing on this epidemic whilst putting its workforce in danger.

In May 2020, reports found that at least twenty meatpacking workers in the US had died of coronavirus, and over 5,000 had become infected. A wave of meatpacking facility closures swept across the country, most of them operated by the largest food manufacturers in America. As a response, Tyson Foods (the world's second-largest meat processor) took out paid adverts in major newspapers to warn that these closures would lead to a limited supply of their product.

Ever mindful to protect big business, the president of the United States, Donald Trump at the time, used the Defense Production Act to mandate meat processing plants remain open during the pandemic.[27] This move basically elevated meat production to an "essential service" and protected the industry from being liable if their employees catch Covid.[28]

Where there is political will, there is a way. This potential could have been used to shift towards sustainable infrastructure that supports our health and protects the planet. Instead, it was used to prop up an industry that does the opposite.

And so it was that meat packing staff found themselves on the frontline, working in factories that offered no social distancing or ventilation systems to keep them safe. A worker at Koch, another one of America's largest meat processors, alleges the company withholds the details of workers who catch Covid and forces staff to wear the same surgical mask over two or three shifts.[29]

According to Michael Osterhold, an infectious disease epidemiologist, deep cleans and surgical masks are not enough to stop the spread of the virus in meatpacking factories.[30] So while lockdowns have kept us all isolated, Covid hotspots like these stayed open. This is yet another example of the industry's blatant disregard for its workers, and the world at large.

While the meat industry waxes lyrical about its contribution to feeding the world, the truth is that it gobbles up resources that could otherwise be shared with people who need them the most. While it speaks of job opportunities and wealth creation, it creates dead-end, poorly paid jobs and an environment riddled with violence, crime, and pollution.

This is an industry that has as little care for people as it does for animals and the planet. The only way we can stop the cycle is to stop feeding into it.

"Hogs get stressed out pretty easy. If you prod them too much, they have heart attacks. If you get a hog in the chute that's had the shit prodded out of him and has a heart attack or refuses to move, you take a meat hook and hook it into his bunghole. You try to do this by clipping the hipbone. Then you drag him backwards. You're dragging these hogs alive, and a lot of times the meat hook rips out of the bunghole. I've seen hams–thighs–completely ripped open. I've also seen intestines come out. If the hog collapses near the front of the chute, you shove the meat hook into his cheek and drag him forward."
Quote from slaughterhouse worker.

"If all the grain currently fed to livestock in the United States were consumed directly by people, the number of people who could be fed would be nearly 800 million."
David Pimentel,
Professor of ecology at Cornell University's
College of Agriculture and Life Sciences[31]

"Meat is an inefficient source of nutrition. Chicken is the most efficient form of meat, but still requires 9 calories of energy to produce 1 calorie of meat and 0.2oz (5g) of protein to produce 0.035oz (1g) of protein. Pork is less efficient, requiring 10 calories of feed to produce 1 calorie of meat. If the world adopted an entirely plant-based diet, current agriculture could easily produce enough food to feed the growing population[32]."

We are currently living with the consequences of the standard Western diet[33] and its reliance on animal products: a world of pandemics, chronic disease, climate collapse, and suffering for humans and the creatures we consume.

Although the truth is confronting, all the crises we face today have solutions that we can be a part of.

We can vote for change three times a day.
The remedy is a more conscious, compassionate lifestyle and diet.

8

LIFE ON THE SPECTRUM

A VEGAN ADVENTURE

"It's important to see carnism and veganism on a spectrum."
Dr Melanie Joy, author of
Why We Eat Pigs, Love Dogs, and Wear Cows[1]

Throughout life, we grapple with a range of nuances within most beliefs, viewpoints, or conditions, whether we were mindful of it or not. We are all somewhere on a number of spectrums, for example, mental health, politics and sexuality—all of us fall somewhere between two extremes. Our position on a spectrum is not fixed, but fluid. Take mental health—depending on circumstances, we might feel depressed, but eventually, we can move out of that and into stability, motivation, and enthusiasm.

I believe we should treat our diets similarly, on a spectrum between carnism (and I'll get into this term in a moment), and veganism. As we gain more knowledge and confidence, we are empowered to move along this spectrum, towards a diet that supports a kinder, healthier, more sustainable world. Here we can reach a place where we are more aligned with our core values.

I always say that veganism, like life, is about the journey and not the destination. I celebrate my unique journey and hope to empower others along the spectrum to a place of compassion and alignment. It is a beautiful feeling of confidence and contentment knowing your lifestyle aligns with your ethics and worldview. I have come a long way from my farming life and I would be honored to share this peace with you and inspire real change.

Now that you have identified your unique mix of driving forces, you can jump into the driving seat and start making changes. Moving along the diet spectrum you will find your sweet spot, and your optimum destination. This is where it can seem tricky or overwhelming. Many people balk at labeling themselves vegan, anxious not to be associated with a seemingly extreme or ascetic movement with its fair share of in-fighting and division.

But I have good news. You don't have to shout your veganism from the rooftops. There isn't a secret handshake or a badge you have to wear. You can make this trip uniquely your own. Find your own way and know where to stop when it feels right. You don't even have to go 100% vegan before you start making a difference. Every step along the path towards veganism is a step in the right direction for you, then animals, and the planet.

In fact, I would argue that 100% vegan does not necessarily mean 100% ethical. After all, with the largest global food retailers jumping onto the vegan bandwagon, you could still be contributing to an industry that profits from animal exploitation. The best-known fast-food outlets now have vegan options. While I support increased choice, veganism is about more than just choosing something because it has a vegan label. Veganism is about asking yourself, "how compassionate, sustainable and kind is my choice?"

It is important to forge your own path and set your own speed and course, rather than simply attaching a label. For example, one of my friends is vegan, but she will eat eggs when she house-sits for friends who keep a couple of hens as pets. The hens are happy, loved, cared for, and their eggs are a byproduct of that, rather than industrial farming, and as such they fit her view of conscious, sustainable eating.

Even some of my strictest vegan friends admit they have moments of weakness. You can be a good vegan and have that slice of your grandmother's shortbread at Christmas. There is no right or wrong. It isn't about being the vegan police, but about YOUR transition towards veganism, and being compassionate and tolerant about other people's choices.

As you move along the dietary spectrum, from carnism towards veganism, make the changes from a place of calm and acceptance. Think of this as a great adventure. There can be many steps between those two points. The important thing is not to get to the other side as quickly as possible, but rather to move in that direction, taking the time to integrate changes into your life for the long haul.

Ultimately, you are already on this journey! By diving into the why's behind veganism, you have already stepped towards a more compassionate lifestyle. Trying out this lifestyle is an exciting opportunity to focus and rethink your daily choices in a new way, not a route to personal perfection.

"The perfect is the enemy of the good."
Voltaire

We must accept that "vegan perfection" is unattainable. To be truly and completely ethical would entail living outside of our current economic and social system. As tempting as life in a wooden cabin in the forest may seem, 99.99% of us cannot escape like this—we have to operate in a world where most of our choices have some negative repercussions. Our smartphones, our energy systems, our cars, our shopping malls, our food delivery services all involve some form of exploitation, some form of environmental damage. To accept this is to free yourself from unrealistic expectations. You alone cannot save the world. But your choices do have repercussions. As we saw in the last chapter, the meat industry is responsible for damage on many levels. It is therefore one of the most pressing areas for change. And it's a change that is relatively straightforward to put into practice, especially if you focus on the journey rather than the destination.

You have the power to change the world
one meal at a time!

Ta-Da!

Going vegan is easy. After all, it can be stripped back to a simple one-step formula. Here it is: stop buying or using products made from animals. What it boils down to is just saying NO animal products "wherever possible and practical." The original definition from over 75 years ago provides us with the big takeaway, the perfect strategy to protect the planet's future, stop harming animals, and improve our emotional and physical wellbeing. In the next chapter, you will find practical tips and tricks to inspire and empower you to start creating your plant-based life.

But first, let's explore the dietary spectrum.

SPECIESISM: ITS A THING.

The assumption of human superiority alongside the belief that animal species are inferior, leading to the exploitation of animals. Speciesist thinking considers that animals are just a means to human ends.[2]

Carnism: The invisible belief system that conditions us to eat certain animals. The term carnism was coined in 2001 by Melanie Joy, a social psychologist and author of Why We Love Dogs, Eat Pigs and Wear Cows. Central to this ideology is the acceptance that meat-eating is natural, normal, and necessary. Carnism classifies certain species of animals as food and accepts practices towards those animals that would be regarded as unacceptable if applied to other species (which is why people can get very emotional about dog-eating festivals while ignoring the same atrocities carried out on pigs and cows).[3]

These are the common rationalizations people use to defend their choice to eat meat...[4]

Natural: Eating meat is written in our biology, we naturally crave meat, our species evolved to eat meat.

Normal: Eating meat is what most people in civilized society do and expect.

Necessary: Eating meat is essential for survival. People need to consume it to be healthy and strong.

It is interesting to note that the three N's of this justification system have also been used to rationalize slavery and sexism. For example, opponents of women's suffrage often appealed to the "necessity" of denying women the vote to prevent "irreparable damage" to the nation, the "natural superiority" of male intelligence, and the "normalcy" of men-only voting as "designed by our forefathers." When scrutinized and challenged, the 3N's ideology collapses, hence the importance of the vegan movement.[5]

THE SPECTRUM—FROM CARNISM TO VEGANISM

Carnism is the opposite of veganism. It is currently the dominant belief system in our culture that influences our dietary choices. It is woven through the fabric of society. We've internalized this ideology and the conflict it creates to such a degree that we can ignore the cruelty needed to sustain our expectation for meat and dairy.

If annual meat consumption doubles from 250 million tons to 500 million tons, as is predicted by the FAO, the system will collapse[6], and so will the world as we know it. We are already on the brink. To avoid this, we all have a part to play. We have to make a conscious choice to move away from animal products and towards plants; away from cruelty, pollution and exploitation, and towards foods that are kind to animals, the planet, and people.

But between carnism and veganism, we have options, room to explore and find our way. One of my favorite expressions is "all those who wander are not lost." We are all wandering somewhere on the spectrum whether we know it or not. There are many variations of diets and many ways of eating.

To achieve the changes needed to sustain our world's population and health, we all need to move towards a plant-based life. In an ideal world, we would all be vegan. I am also a vegan realist: I accept the world can't go vegan overnight (but I will keep trying!). So I think it is time to get real and recognize that we can all still make a dramatic difference to our world by reducing our consumption of animal products. At every step of the dietary spectrum, there is scope for you to have a positive impact.

Take a look at the spectrum below—where are you now, and where do you want to be?

A REBEL VEGAN is aware of the impact of food,
and wants to make sustainable, compassionate choices.

CARNISM TO VEGANISM SPECTRUM

- **Carnism:** The dominant diet that's been developing since the agrarian revolution. A carnist diet includes meat, fish, eggs and dairy. These items are consumed daily, often several times a day. The standard Western diet[7] is a carnist diet.

- **Flexitarianism:** A flexitarian diet focuses on a higher intake of plant foods while reducing meat. Animal products are viewed as a side dish rather than the main event. The Blue Zones diets are flexitarian. Although they include a small amount of meat, fish and dairy, they are heavily dependent on whole foods like vegetables, pulses, grains, nuts, and seeds.

- **Pescetarianism:** A pescetarian diet combines fish and seafood with plant-foods such as vegetables, beans, fruits, and grains. Pescetarianism can also sometimes include eggs and dairy.

- **Ovo-lacto-vegetarianism:** The most common form of vegetarianism. Meat and fish do not feature in this diet, but eggs and dairy do.

- **Lacto-vegetarianism:** Lacto-vegetarians consume dairy, but no eggs, meat or fish.

- **Ovo-vegetarianism:** Ovo-vegetarians consume eggs, but no meat, fish or dairy products.

- **Veganism (also known as plant-based):** Vegans do not consume any meat, fish, dairy, eggs, honey, or other products derived from animals. They try to avoid any products that may have involved animal exploitation or abuse.

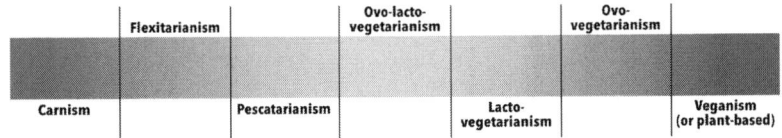

NB: For me, veganism and plant-based are interchangeable. However, within the vegan movement there's some discussion and debate about safeguarding the term vegan. Some vegans consider the term plant-based too open and more about the diet or health over the wider lifestyle or ethical concerns. I want to foster unity and focus on our shared values. I think these are semantics, as ultimately we're all trying to move towards a more compassionate life. We're all in this together.

Wherever you are between carnism and veganism, you can have a positive impact on the environment and your health. Once you begin moving towards veganism, you'll find that you naturally keep going. The benefits you will experience will make it easy to carry on. That sense of wellbeing and the confidence that your core values and lifestyle are aligned is profound. But you must begin with the acceptance that your pace may differ from other people, and that's okay. The more compassion you can show yourself on this journey, the easier it will be to transition towards being fully vegan.

I hope the information in this book is transformational, but I am not here to preach or guilt-trip anyone. Your path is unique and doesn't have to arrive at 100% veganism to make a difference. In fact, you can begin making a difference wherever you are on this spectrum by infusing the principles of veganism into each aspect of your life—compassion, sustainability, and ethics. That means if you choose to move towards veganism by going flexitarian, pescatarian or vegetarian, you do so while sourcing products that are as ethical, sustainable and humane as possible, for example by ditching the big suppliers and choosing to shop from local, independent businesses.

Do not be so rigid that you give up. I can't tell you how many people have tried veganism for a few weeks, only to throw in the towel because it was "too hard" or they were "so hungry" or got "bored of eating the same meal over and over again." This can happen when you switch to veganism too quickly, without proper planning, or if you blindly follow somebody else's protocol instead of sitting down to work out how to make this new lifestyle work for your body and your circumstances.

The trick to make changes stick is to have a clear plan of action, take it slow, and accept it is a journey with twists and turns. It might take you a few attempts to find the right vegan cheese, vegan burger, or plant milk alternative. It might take a few months before you have enough plant-based dishes in your repertoire. There may be moments when you revert to something familiar because you're in a rush, stressed or socializing. This is okay. It is better to allow yourself the space to make mistakes and keep going, rather than aiming for perfection and giving up. Don't forget that you're not just changing your diet, but rethinking your traditions, upbringing, and belief system!

MY VEGAN JOURNEY

Like most of you, I was raised a meat-eater. In fact, I was raised on a farm and at the opposite end of the diet spectrum to where I find myself today. As a child, I kept my head down and accepted the world around me as the natural order and how things are done. So it's been my personal pilgrimage along the spectrum to find my happy place of contentment and alignment as an out and proud vegan.

I first embraced the plant-based lifestyle at a monastery hidden in a lush jungle in north Vietnam. My first weeks as a vegan were easy as I was within monastery walls and the monks made all my meals. They showed me the importance of balance and simplicity in food. I was dipping my toe into a whole food plant-based diet before I had even heard of that concept.

I felt so revitalized that I decided to maintain the diet after leaving the monastery, however re-establishing myself as a vegan while living life on the road was tricky. I had my favorite haunts dotted around Asia, but they were used to serving me Bò lac (shaking beef) or Gà den (grilled chicken), or even Tiêt canh (blood pudding). I needed a total rethink, and this was a daunting prospect.

While touring the world, I had built up a loyal network of connections with quirky locally-run restaurants whose owners had become friends. They knew all my favorite dishes and liked to indulge me as a loyal patron. I remember walking into a small town I'd not been to in over a year, and wondering if anyone would remember me.

I needn't have worried. I hadn't walked ten feet along the ramshackle main road before screams of excitement sounded, and I was grabbed off the street by old friends and thrust into the best seat in their restaurant. They disappeared into the kitchen without a word, and soon proudly presented me with my favorite curry and a freshly opened coconut. The curry contained their best meat, as a gesture of friendship, and I needed to figure out how to respect our connection while still honoring my new values.

The concept of veganism was alien to many. There is no word for vegan or plant-based in many Asian languages, and lots of people laughed at what they thought of as a crazy diet. They told me I was skinny and needed to fatten up. Old friends would offer to kill a chicken just for me!

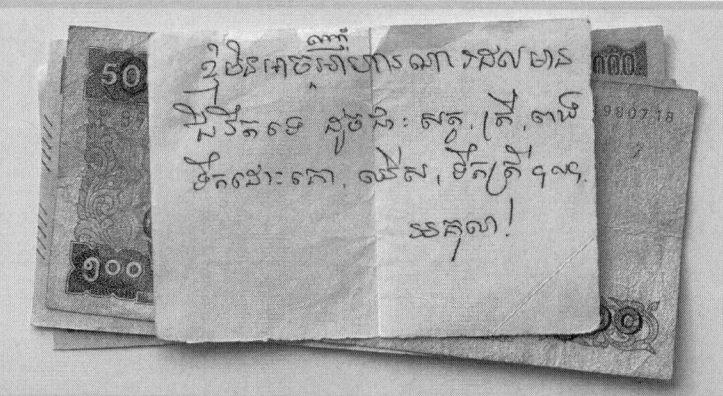

I wrote cards in each local language to show the foods I couldn't eat and photocopied them to hand out to friends, waiters, and restaurant owners. Often I would go into the kitchen and explain, or get behind the counters and help adapt my favorite dishes. This always sparked a wider conversation about vegan philosophy and the driving forces for my dramatic shift in lifestyle. When done right—when it remained a conversation rather than an opportunity for one-upmanship—these conversations were inspiring, fascinating, and a unique opportunity to laugh and bond with my old friends.

I learned that many of the so-called "classic dishes" were Westernized versions, with meat added to appeal to travelers. Originally, meat wasn't in every meal. Their intricate and world-famous flavors were developed with plants alone.

Becoming vegan never restricted me. On the contrary, it opened up my world. My connections grew stronger. My friends in all those little cafes around the world grew to respect my choices and even veganized their menus to appeal to a new class of traveler. I think our open conversations also helped some to rethink their increasingly meat-centric diets.

These days, when I return, they still jump up, excited to feed me their latest vegan creation or discovery. We are on the map!

"You are not the vegan police."
REBEL VEGAN

VEGAN POLICE ON THE STREETS:
COMPASSION TOWARDS OTHER VEGANS

The optimum diet, when it comes to health, animal welfare, and the environment, is a fully plant-based diet. Having said that, any movement towards this ideal is a positive that should be supported and celebrated. Unfortunately, I have all too often seen vegans judge and condemn anyone who isn't 100% vegan. We are *REBEL VEGANS*, not the vegan police. Veganism should be a judgment-free zone. We must welcome and encourage all who come to veganism, wherever they are on the spectrum.

We are all in this together. One of the saddest things for me is the conflict and arguing I see happening among vegans. We are all on the dietary spectrum, and we need to support each other, not criticize or break into cliquey groups. Our voices are louder when we stand together and our message is stronger as a united movement.

While we're busy fighting among ourselves, we're going against the core principle of veganism: compassion. Being a *REBEL VEGAN* is also about creating a welcoming and safe space for others to join us. And that won't happen if we criticize and judge ourselves or others for being "not vegan enough."

Live by your rules, be confident in your choices,
and kind towards other people's choices.

Everything—even you—can be veganized. Even with that in mind, it is important that you allow yourself to move through the spectrum with grace and at your own pace. Perhaps you will be determined to throw all animal products out of the window and never buy them again. Or you will be more measured and slow in your approach, taking it week by week and slowly phasing out your usual meals with plant-based alternatives. It does not matter. Wherever you are, I celebrate that you are here. What matters is that you are on your way. In my book, that makes you a *REBEL VEGAN* and you have a seat at my table.

However you choose to navigate this, you must set an example. Veganism is not about being perfect, it is about being compassionate.

That means extending your compassion to include all earthlings, including fellow humans still involved in carnism.

Put it this way: judging or shaming somebody's actions never results in positive change. It just puts people's backs up and keeps people polarized. After all, how do you feel when others judge or criticize you? You inspire positive change with your energy when you stand in your authentic truth with tolerance and understanding.

That does not mean you condone the act of eating meat, it means you understand that the person doing so is currently enmeshed in a pervasive ideology. Let's embrace and celebrate everyone's efforts to create a better world, one meal at a time.

MOVING ALONG THE DIETARY SPECTRUM

You are a REBEL VEGAN,
informed and motivated to create your best life.
Remember that like life, veganism is about the journey.
Enjoy.

There is no rulebook—no one way— to do vegan. With the strategies in the next two chapters, you can begin to create your unique plant-based lifestyle. I always say veganism is a journey, not a destination - so let's enjoy the ride!

How committed or chilled you are, and wherever you find your sweet spot on the dietary spectrum, is entirely your choice to make. Only you know your goals, only you can align your ethics, and only you can find the best way to navigate this brave new world. Don't be afraid of others judging you—just do you.

Yes, you will face challenges. You may experience friends and family questioning your choices, you may stumble and make mistakes, you may move at a different pace than others. Wherever you are on the spectrum, and wherever you're going, you do not need to label yourself, just align your newly awakened beliefs and motivations with your everyday life.

I believe the path to veganism is like a homecoming—to return to your original compassionate self.

You become who you were always meant to be.
Welcome home.

9

REBEL VEGAN STARTER KIT

CREATING YOUR OWN PLANT-BASED LIFE

*The best way to make a difference in the world
is to start by making a difference in your own life.*
Julia Louis-Dreyfus

Treat this chapter as your starter kit to establishing and maintaining your plant-based life. In this chapter, I want to confirm your motivations with a concise summary of the benefits of going vegan, and give you a blueprint for starting your vegan journey.

No matter how far along you are on the diet spectrum, as you move towards being more plant-based, you are improving your health, saving animals, and helping fight climate change. It's not about perfection, the focus is better placed on living your best life and doing the right thing. When you believe in something, it is so much easier to make the changes you need to align with that mission.

BENEFITS FOR EARTHLINGS:

1. You spare the lives of many animals:
Maybe this one is obvious, but with 70 billion land animals being bred, farmed, and slaughtered each year, your choice to leave them off your plate is the first step to ending animal suffering. Not to mention the millions of animals you'll spare from being made homeless due to deforestation. You also help prevent species extinction by eliminating the need for livestock and feed crops.

2. You stand up for human rights:
Most factory farm workers are exploited and underpaid. They are denied breaks and have to work in unimaginable conditions doing jobs that damage the body and soul. By going vegan, you stop contributing to this industry and stand up for human rights.

3. You help fight world hunger:
According to the United Nations World Food Program, 690 million people go to bed hungry every night.[1] The more people transition to a plant-based diet, the more farmland could be used to grow grains and vegetables to feed the world, rather than feed farm animals for the meat industry.

4. You stand up against torture and for a kinder world:
There is nothing kind about what happens in factory farms. Not eating meat means you no longer contribute to an industry that depends on the torture and slaughter of sentient beings.

You must be the change you want to see in the world.
Mahatma Gandhi

BENEFITS FOR THE WORLD:

5. Conserving water:

It takes 1,000 gallons (3,785 liters) of water to produce 1 gallon (3.7 liters) of milk. It takes 4 million gallons (15 million liters) of water to produce a ton of beef. On the other hand, it takes 85,000 gallons (321,760 liters) of water to produce a ton of vegetables. By going vegan, you can save 219,000 gallons (829,000 liters) of water every year.

Animal agriculture is notoriously polluting to freshwater reserves as well as the oceans due to the toxic run-off and leaks from CAFO waste pits. When you go vegan, you are also helping to keep our water clean.

6. Protecting the soil:

Animal agriculture depletes fertile soils. Not only because of the high level of chemicals in waste sprayed onto fields, but also due to deforestation. On the other hand, growing a large variety of plants and trees can reverse these effects, helping to remineralize and renourish the soil.

7. Reducing carbon emissions:

According to Nobel Prize-winning physicist and president of the American Association for the Advancement of Science, Steven Chu, "If cattle and dairy were a country, they would have more greenhouse gas emissions than the entire EU 28."[2] According to Cornell University, producing animal protein takes eight times more fossil fuel energy than producing plants.[3]

When you follow a vegan diet, you produce the equivalent of 50% less carbon dioxide and 1/11th of the oil compared to a meat-eater.[4]

8. Land use

It takes 1/6th of an acre to feed one person for one year on a vegan diet. It takes 3 times more land to feed a vegetarian. It takes 18 times more land to feed a meat eater.[5]

1.5 acres of land can produce 37,000 pounds (16,783 kilos) of plant-based food, or just 375 pounds (124 kilos) of beef. [6]

BENEFITS FOR YOUR HEALTH:

If you desire to make a difference in the world,
you must be different from the world.
Elaine S. Dalton

9. You will lose weight:
The standard Western diet[7] is implicated in the global obesity epidemic. By switching to a vegan diet, you avoid sources of saturated fat and toxins that contribute to weight gain, thereby helping you reach your ideal weight.

10. You will live longer and feel healthier:
A vegan diet is richer in nutrients that help protect against disease. But you don't even have to go 100% plant-based to experience these benefits. Studies show that even flexitarians live longer, healthier lives.[8]

11. You will protect yourself from chronic diseases:
The standard Western diet[9] increases your risk of metabolic syndrome. This syndrome is characterized by the so-called "deadly quartet"—abdominal obesity, high blood sugar, high cholesterol and high blood pressure.[10] If you follow a plant-based diet, you reduce your risk of metabolic syndrome.

12. You will experience a happier, more peaceful mood:
The standard Western diet[11] is associated with a higher risk of mood disorders. On the other hand, a plant-based diet significantly improves depression, anxiety and productivity.[12] And there's a lot to be said for the peace-of-mind that comes from knowing that you are taking action to help the world.

A PERSON WHO EATS A VEGAN DIET SAVES, PER DAY:[13]
- - 1,100 gallons (4,163 liters) of water.
- - 45 pounds (23 kilos) of grain.
- - 30 square feet (9.1 square meters) of forested land.
- - 20 pounds (10 kilos) of CO_2.
- - One animal's life.

THE FIRST STEP: PLANNING

"If You Fail to Plan, You Are Planning to Fail"
Benjamin Franklin

So now you are motivated, the question is...how to begin? As much as going vegan is relatively straight-forward, it is also challenging. Firstly, because it can be difficult to change your behaviors when the behaviors of those around you remain the same. You might be the first vegan in your family or friend group, which means you will have to make an effort to stand your ground (see chapter 7 for vegan comebacks). Secondly, going vegan can be challenging because you are breaking the habit of a lifetime.

Habits run deep. Most of us grew up eating meat and dairy and not giving it a second thought. Our reflexes, taste buds, and habitual patterns will work against us making these positive changes. But with creativity and courage, we can challenge these ingrained beliefs and traditions.

We do this by creating new traditions and new habits that are kinder and more sustainable. Finding and strengthening your personal why—that mix of powerful driving forces that turned you towards this path in the first place—will help you face these challenges and any bumps in the road.

But motivation will only take you so far. Failure to plan is planning to fail. So the first step on your journey along the vegan spectrum is to plan ahead! My favorite way to do this is to journal about it, but you can also just follow along or find a method that resonates with you. Below, you will find my step by step process. I hope it helps inspire your Rebel Vegan journey.

1. GET SUPER CLEAR ON YOUR WHY:

You've read the driving forces. You had your own motivations beforehand. What are your reasons for going vegan? It might be your health, or that you no longer want to contribute to a cruel and polluting industry, it could be that you cannot stand the thought of what is happening to our planet because of our food choices. A clear why will help you stay strong and stick to your choices when the going gets tough.

2. VISUALIZE THE BENEFITS:

How will you feel as you make these changes? What are you going to achieve? What are the benefits you will experience as you transition to a plant-based way of life? A clear vision of the positive outcomes of your choice will help cement your decision and support your goals.

3. BE AWARE OF YOUR CHALLENGES:

Write about (or think about) the obstacles that could get in your way and how you will navigate them. For example, if your go-to coffee shop doesn't have vegan options, are there cafes nearby that do? Or if you tend to get hungry mid-morning and reach for a shop-bought muffin, can you prepare vegan snacks in advance so you don't get caught out? If and when people question your choices, how will you respond? Where might you be prepared to compromise, and where are you not prepared to compromise (for example: if your mum has made a fish stew, versus if your friends try to drag you to a kebab shop after a night out).

4. PLAN FOR CHANGES:

Make a plan and stick to it. I like to take it one week at a time. What changes will you make in the first, second, third, and fourth week? Start small. Do it step by step and build from there. For example, it might feel overwhelming to go completely vegan from week 1. But you could decide that the first week will focus on finding plant-based alternatives to your usual dairy foods, and the second week will have two or three plant-based days. Or you might start by sampling vegan "meats" to find the ones that you enjoy.

5. READY, SET, VEGANIZE:

We are in an exciting time, vegan-wise. There is literally a vegan option for everything now: milk, yogurt, butter, mince meat, chicken, burgers, cheese, fish. Any dish you enjoy can be made vegan. Get online and start looking for vegan versions of your favorite foods.

Remember this is not a race! It's about building in lasting change, so go at your own pace, and just do your best. Before you know it, you'll have transitioned to a way of eating that supports your health, animal welfare, and the planet.

We have covered the practicalities, so now let's learn some tips and tricks to start putting your new lifestyle into action.

For a more detailed approach to Nutrition and how to live a Vegan lifestyle please see book two in the *REBEL VEGAN* range—*REBEL VEGAN LIFE*: **Full Nutritional and Beginners Guide.**

If you can visualize it,
you can veganize it.
REBEL VEGAN

EGO

10

THE HOW

Q: What's the hardest thing about being vegan?
A: Waking up to milk the almonds.

Wherever you are, I want to support you to follow your unique path towards your sweet spot on the spectrum.

Our food choices are emotional, irrational, and wrapped up in our childhoods and culture. As a *REBEL VEGAN*, you need to be prepared to challenge old beliefs and change your lifestyle. Although this journey is challenging at times, it will ultimately bring much joy, make a positive impact on the planet, on the animals, and on your health, with every single bite. In the last chapter, I shared my strategy to plan your plant-based life. In this chapter, I'm going to share a few tips and tricks to help you on the journey:

1. **Be prepared and motivated:** Use this book as your springboard and reference to start a healthier and more sustainable life. Think of it as a bible to return to and renew your inspiration. Use the resources section in the Appendix to find further information, inspiration, recipes, and support groups.

2. **Go at your own pace and go your own way:** There is no one way to do this. Don't compare yourself to others or feel pressured to conform to someone else's idea of what you should be doing. Celebrate your accomplishments, no matter how small.

3. **Be open-minded and push yourself outside—or to the limits of—your comfort zone:** A negative attitude will guarantee failure. View this as an incredible opportunity to explore new foods, tastes, restaurants, and cultures. Keep it fun! It's an adventure that also saves the planet!

4. **Don't judge or become the vegan police:** It's hard not to become zealous with your newfound health and wisdom and want to shout it from the rooftops. But if you want to make the change and keep your friends while you're at it, you have to realize that not everybody is at the same point in their life, and not everybody has the same value system. And that is okay. As a *REBEL VEGAN*, you inspire and lead by example.

5. **Be prepared to be questioned and challenged:** When it comes to something so ingrained and sensitive as food, everyone thinks they are an expert and will come at you with unsolicited advice that may require a lot of gritted teeth, filtering, and magnanimity. No one cared when I ate meat. Now I'm vegan, everyone has an opinion on my health! Try to stay strong and positive, and be a bigger person. They can't argue with how great you look!

6. **Find your tribe for community and support:** You are not alone on this journey, so reach out to others for mutual support and connection. This is also part of the adventure. I look back and it astonishes me that something I initially found so isolating has now come full circle and created a new community I cherish. One of the top reasons many people give up or fall back into old habits is isolation.[1] See this as a great opportunity to open up your world and connect with others in the plant-based community. (See our Facebook groups in resources.)

7. **Make starchy vegetables and whole grains the foundation of your diet:** Despite popular myth, even the most hipster of vegans can't survive on kale salad alone! You need to eat enough healthy calories to satisfy your appetite (a pound of spinach has only 92 calories), otherwise you will fall back into old habits. This means putting starchy vegetables, whole grains, and plant protein at the center of your plate: potatoes, sweet potatoes, pumpkins, carrots, rice, quinoa, buckwheat, oats, beans, lentils, and soy products. I knew I could happily be a full time vegan when I tasted plant-based burger options and made sweet potato lasagna!

8. **Pack your kitchen with tasty vegan staples:** This way you'll always have something healthy to whip up and snack on. Some of the things I always have on hand are hummus, trail mix, granola, peanut butter (to spread on oat crackers, sourdough, or to have with an apple), canned beans (that way you can quickly add protein to your salads or blend up a quick bean dip), dried herbs and spices (so you can sauté vegetables into a delicious stir fry you can serve with noodles, or make a quick curry or stew), several types of grains (I always have rice, dried noodles and pasta in my cupboards), nuts and seeds (the easiest snack in the world! Roast them and keep them in an airtight jar ready to grab when you're feeling hungry), frozen fruit (I put frozen blueberries in

my muesli and use them to make smoothies), plant-based milk (for those mourning flat whites and afternoon cups of tea). The staples you choose will depend on your unique tastes and requirements, but ensuring you have a well stocked vegan pantry will guarantee your success as a *REBEL VEGAN*.

9. **Make a simple pasta dish more nutritious:** Dried pasta is usually vegan, while fresh pasta is commonly made with eggs. There are also some amazing lentil and chickpea pastas out there to try! To make your pasta dishes more filling and nutritious, switch to a bean or high quality, whole grain pasta made with ancient grains (for example buckwheat, brown rice or spelt). Add more protein with tempeh, tofu, beans, chickpeas, or hummus. Add some healthy fats with avocado, seeds, or nuts. You can also add creaminess with oat, almond, or soy cream. Add antioxidant-packed veggies like broccoli, purple cabbage, mushrooms, or spinach. This meal is much more nutritionally dense and will keep you full longer, versus a stand-alone bowl of pasta.

10. **Smoothies:** If you don't want to blend on a daily basis, you can blend or cold press your favorite berries, greens, and fruits, then freeze in zip-lock bags, ready to go. To ensure your smoothies keep you full until lunch, turn them into smoothie bowls topped with granola, nuts, seeds, and coconut shreds. Or you can add a source of protein to the smoothies, such as chia seeds, hemp seeds, nut butter, or plant protein powder.

11. **Have food on standby:** This way you don't have to succumb to take-aways. Freeze some home-cooked or store-bought vegan meals for those lazy or stressful days.

12. **Time to tool up:** You don't want your new diet to be time-consuming or take over your life. I recommend a pressure cooker. It will slash cooking time, preserve food nutrient value, and has multiple cooking functions. A decent blender is also a good idea (for smoothies, but also vegan mayo, cheesecakes, energy balls, soups, etc).

13. **Be ready to feel lighter and stay regular:** Your diet is about to get healthier with more nutrients and fiber. Meat products contain negligible amounts of vitamins and no fiber whatsoever. Fiber is what keeps your bowel movements regular. This is essential, as it is one of the ways your body gets rid of toxins. Eating enough plant fiber helps prevent (and even reverse) colon and bowel cancers.[2] What's more, fibre keeps you fuller, so expect to experience better appetite control and healthy weight loss.

14. **Veganize your favorite dishes:** There are incredible replacement options available, and hundreds, if not thousands, of vegan cookbooks out

there. Enjoy the journey, find new flavors, and have fun experimenting. There is a plant-based version of everything, whatever your preferences. This change is not restrictive, but opens up your world.

15. **Plan ahead:** Don't rely on pre-made or junk foods. Oreos and French fries are technically vegan, I know, but they won't deliver the health benefits that whole foods do. Make a plan so you can make (and freeze) home-cooked meals and have healthy vegan snacks on standby. Learn a few simple go-to recipes. Stock your fridge with your favorites, like vegan pizza or burgers, for those weak moments. Explore and find your new signature dish. Mine was jackfruit curry!

16. **Support local restaurants and become a vegan social butterfly:** Post-Covid, we lost a lot of restaurants, but new vegan ones are opening up everywhere. Let's support and champion them! (See the resource list in the Appendix and download the HappyCow app!)

17. **Don't forget supplements:** The only essential nutrient missing from a vegan diet is B12. Find a good quality, food-grown supplement to ensure you get enough. Some people also choose to top up on iron and Omega-3 as well. In addition, a wide-spectrum multi-vitamin will help you keep your nutrient levels topped up.

18. **Don't sweat the small stuff:** Try to keep focused on the bigger picture and your goal of transitioning to a more plant-based life. Don't get too lost in sourcing only organic, reading every label, or knowing everything, because this can become stressful and make anyone give up. The moment any diet stops being fun is the moment you begin to think it might not be worth it. By becoming aware and more plant-based, you are already making a bold move to improve your life and the world around you. Be kind to yourself!

19. **Give yourself time to adjust as your knowledge and willpower grow:** Your thoughts and taste buds evolve as your horizons and options expand. Taste is acquired, and soon you will start to crave all things plant-based. Many people find one thing hard to give up, like cheese. If you need to fall back on that while you transition and find a vegan alternative, that's okay. You are a *REBEL VEGAN*, walking your own path, still creating a better life and making a positive impact.

20. **Don't let perfection get in the way of progress:** You will, by mistake or design, eat animal products again. When accidents happen, try to forgive, learn, and move on!

21. **Don't get disheartened:** There will be bumps in the road, but stay focused on your new life. Veganism is a journey, not a destination. Enjoy the ride!

Q & A: COMMON QUESTIONS FROM NEWBIE VEGANS

Q: Why does vegan cheese taste bad?
A: It hasn't been tested on mice.

WILL I EVER STOP CRAVING MEAT?

I never miss meat anymore. I always say our taste buds are fickle with short term memory. Basically they will crave what they are most used to. Switching to a plant-based diet is very similar to moving to a far flung country after growing up on your mother's traditional cooking. You have to give yourself time to acclimatize and discover new flavors.

Another thing to remember is that most packaged foods are hyper-sweet, mega-salty, or over-flavored thanks to all the artificial additives, and this causes our taste buds to become desensitized and overwhelmed. But you can retrain your tastebuds to appreciate and crave new foods simply by eating new foods. With every bite, your tastebuds learn to savor something else.

Give yourself time, and it will happen - usually over a few weeks or months. I missed old fashioned cheese for a year, and now I turn my nose up at it. Time and commitment will open up your world.

CAN MY PETS BE VEGAN?

Cats are carnivores, natural predators, and the opposite of vegans. Their physiology demands they eat meat. There are stories of cat lovers creating carefully fortified vegan cat foods and raising healthy cats. However, it is okay to accept your cat's nature and feed it with meat products. I am not the vegan police, and you are still a *REBEL VEGAN* and a good person. On the other hand, dogs are omnivores like humans, which means they can thrive on a plant-based diet. There are many healthy vegan dog food options out there. Actually, the oldest living dog, Brambles, was a *REBEL VEGAN* and lived 27 years![3]

Dogs need protein, but protein is not exclusively found in meat. Protein is made from amino acids, which are found in plant foods. The only reason there are amino acids in meat is because animals (cows, chickens, etc.) eat plants. Meat-based dog foods also contain antibiotic and medication residues, so much so that it is considered "unfit for human consumption."

Our pets are part of the family, let's feed them like we love them.

DO I NEED TO GET RID OF MY LEATHER SHOES AND BELTS?

How far you want to go with your veganism is a personal choice. If animal welfare is one of your driving factors, you probably won't want to buy any more leather products. What you do with the items you bought in the past is up to you. The leather I already had in my pre-vegan closet, I consider vintage and have held on to. However, knowing the violent system that produced these items, I find I don't want to wear them anymore.

The good news is that you don't have to buy leather shoes and belts anymore. There are great faux leather and faux fur options now. Let's support those brands.

DO I NEED TO BUY ORGANIC FOODS?

Small-scale organic produce is better for the environment and contains more nutrients than produce grown conventionally. However, it is important that you do whatever feels right and is within your budget.

You have already made brave choices that will have a huge impact on your health and the environment. I suggest you do not take on the world all at once! If you choose to go organic, I suggest finding a local vegetable box scheme and independent suppliers. The main thing to remember if you aren't buying organic is to thoroughly wash your fresh produce to remove pesticide residues. You can find vegetable wash in most health food stores, or make your own using baking soda, lemon juice and water.

ISN'T SOY BAD FOR YOUR HEALTH?

Is soy good or bad? There has been a lot of conflicting information about soy. Much of this controversy revolves around a supposed link between soy and higher levels of the hormone estrogen. Scare-stories about soy-cause man-boobs are guaranteed to send many men running to the meat aislE, but these links have been fully refuted and debunked.

Firstly, soy does not have an adverse effect on men. Quite the opposite: soy products can even prevent cancer. A review of 47 studies and reports found that neither soy nor soy products affect testosterone levels in men.[4] Another analysis of 14 studies showed that eating soy reduced the risk of prostate cancer by 26%.[5]

Soy is a legume (like chickpeas, peanuts, and pinto beans). It is packed with plant protein, fiber, and vitamins (including calcium). According to the Physicians Committee for Responsible Medicine, soy products offer many benefits, such as reducing the risk of breast cancer and chronic inflammation, and improving bone and heart health.[6]

Of course, discernment is necessary. Health benefits come from consuming whole soy foods, such as tofu, tempeh, soy milk, and soy miso, rather than processed soy products. The more processed a food, the less nutritious it is likely to be.

WHAT'S WRONG WITH EATING HONEY?

Honey is produced by bees for bees. When we harvest honey for our consumption, we are putting the bees' health in danger. According to the Vegan Society, honey production is exploitative.[7]

Bees will visit up to 1,500 flowers to fill their "honey stomach," a separate stomach containing enzymes that break down the nectar into honey. This is deposited in the hive, where "house bees" complete the honey making process. In her lifetime (about a month), each bee will produce a twelfth of a teaspoon of honey. This honey is essential to the hive's wellbeing, providing energy and micronutrients.

In commercial beekeeping, all the honey is taken away and replaced with sugar or glucose syrup , which lacks nutrients and impacts the bee's health. To remedy this, the hives are sometimes doused in antibiotics. Just like in animal farming, conventional beekeepers selectively breed honey bees to increase their productivity. This creates genetically narrow populations of bees that are more prone to diseases. These diseases spread to other pollinators, like native bumblebees. Antibiotics are used to keep parasites at bay. If hives develop parasitic infections, they are often burned with the bees inside.[8]

Another common practice is for hives to be culled post-harvest to keep costs down, and for the queen bee's wings to be clipped to stop her leaving the hive and creating a new colony (since this would decrease productivity and profit).[9]

Honey bees are highly intelligent creatures with complex social systems. What's more, their survival is essential to our survival on earth (over a third of our food depends on pollinators like bees). At the end of the day, we need them more than they need us!

The good news is there are some fantastic honey alternatives out there, whether you want to cook with it, add it to your tea, or drizzle it onto sourdough toast. Maple syrup, rice syrup, molasses, agave syrup, date syrup, not to mention some wonderful vegan honeys!

I am so vegan, I don't even call my boyfriend Honey!

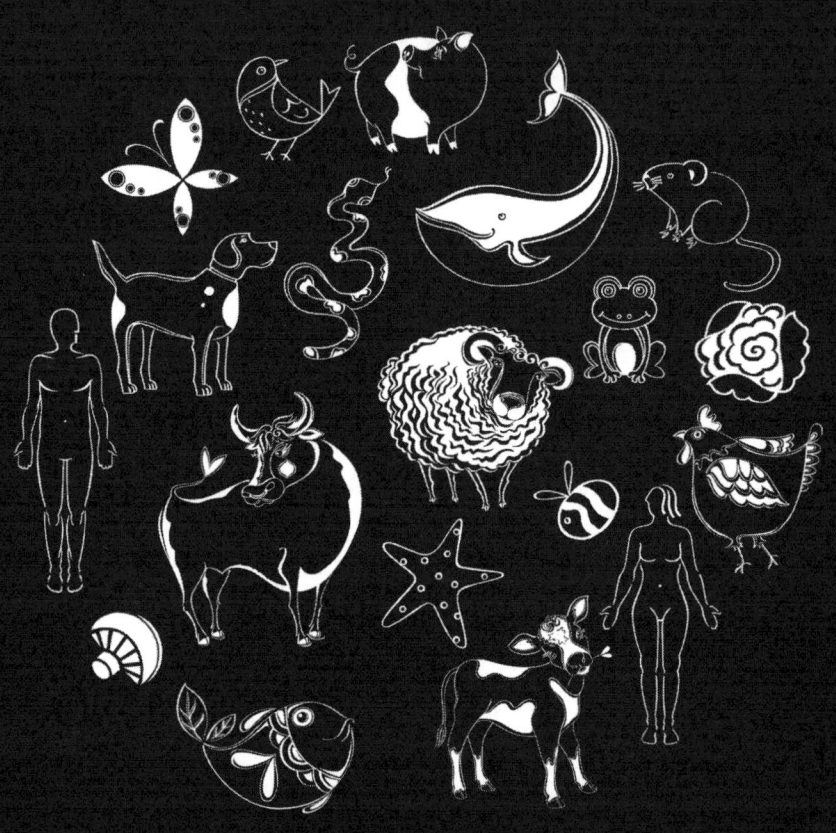

ECO

11

EMPOWERMENT

COMEBACKS FOR CONFRONTING SKEPTICISM

*"People eat meat and think
they will become as strong as an ox,
forgetting that the ox eats grass."*
Pino Caruso[1]

Sometimes you need to rebel, to fight for what's right. So get ready to ruffle feathers just by living authentically as the best version of you—a healthy, confident advocate for compassionate living.

I find it endlessly fascinating that being vegan can cause such consternation and conflict. A vegan arriving at a dinner party can create tension before they even say a word. I believe it has to do with the unspoken belief system we all grow up with that eating meat is normal, natural, some kind of "right."

A vegan's very existence challenges this assumption, and it can be uncomfortable and confronting to some. This kind of moral schizophrenia allows people to love their pets, but eat meat anyway—to say they care for animals while supporting industries that make no secret of their mistreatment of animals.

This is part of a wider problem. We are forced, in today's world, to shut down or tune out our natural human compassion in order to live within a system that produces such pain and injustice. A child would never want an animal to be in pain. As we grow up, we absorb an ideology that makes it normal, whether we think animals were put on this earth purely for us to use at will, or whether we believe in the "survival of the fittest" model, where humans are at the top of the food chain, so must consume animals lest they take over the world.

Just by turning up somewhere, vegans shine a light on this cognitive dissonance, this moral schizophrenia. You are a rebel, so get ready to cause a stir!

Even as the most discreet vegan who doesn't use the V-word, you still must be prepared to be challenged on your personal and philosophical choices. It can involve a lot of forced smiling and magnanimity to have to continuously explain yourself—to come out again and again. Even if you are determined not to say a word about your diet, someone will bring it up. This chapter is about equipping you with the tools and information to answer anything that's thrown at you, and answer with compassion, understanding, and strength.

I have experienced many responses to my veganism. Very often, whoever I'm speaking to is quick to tell me that they don't eat much meat anyway. This points to a fear of judgment, as well as an understanding that meat-eating is not all that good for anyone. If you are faced with this response, celebrate it. Tell the person that it's wonderful they don't eat much meat, because if everyone reduced their reliance on meat, we would already be heading in the right direction on many pressing issues. You might just inspire someone to make brave choices and continue further on their plant-based journey.

But a lot of the time, the response isn't quite as neutral. I've had people telling me that my muscles will waste away due to lack of protein, that there's no way I'll get enough nutrients, crazy claims that veganism is just as bad for the planet, and what about plants, don't they have feelings too? (See below!)

BEFORE EMPOWERMENT: UNDERSTANDING

"You can, you should,
and if you are brave enough to start, you will."
Stephen King

Before we get into debunking some of the misinformation and skepticism you may face, let's explore where this conflict and push-back comes from. I love to watch and understand the dynamics at play, like being a vegan anthropologist!

I believe at the core of this conflict is the assumption or sense that eating meat is some kind of basic human right that vegans are trying to take away. "They're taking our meat" is almost as divisive as "they're taking our jobs" or "they're taking our guns." Meat has become a symbol of resistance against "wokeness" and progressive thinking. Veganism is regarded as another snowflake fad, peddled by a bunch of new-age hippies who have no respect for tradition and freedoms.

Eating meat has become aligned with a kind of toxic conservative alpha-masculinity. Donald Trump famously loves junk food and well-done steak with ketchup. Men's rights advocate Jordan Peterson is known for his beef and salt diet. There's even a subset of cryptocurrency enthusiasts who call themselves bitcoin carnivores. Remember Gatis Lagzdins? Many vegans know him as that guy who turns up at vegan festivals and eats raw meat (stunts have included a squirrel and a pig's head) as a way of raising awareness of the dangers of malnutrition from going vegan.[2] Before turning his attention to people trying to live a more compassionate life, Lagzdin was best known for promoting racist ideology and right-wing conspiracies on his YouTube channel.[3] Social justice warriors are routinely called "soy boy", "cuck", and "beta" in alt-right circles, terms designed to mock their perceived lack of masculinity. This is echoed by a study entitled "It ain't easy eating greens: Evidence bias towards vegetarians and vegans from both source and target", which found that respondents with a right-wing background and holding rigid gender values see vegans as alarmingly subversive and deserving of mockery.[4]

Full disclosure: I wasn't always vegan. For most of my life, I had my head in the sand with regards to diet. In my meat-eating days, I didn't (want to) understand what motivated people to go meatless, and I also poked fun at vegans. I didn't question my behavior at the time. It's only now, looking back, that I see my derision was caused by discomfort. Just by being present, vegans shone a light on choices I subconsciously knew to be toxic. And so I would have a little dig, I would get a little defensive. I am not proud of this. Maybe you have done the same? It's okay. No judgment here. These are natural reactions when faced with an uncomfortable truth.

It's time to embrace your choices and celebrate being a *REBEL VEGAN* who takes new paths, challenges the status quo, and embraces a new way to live. As a *REBEL VEGAN*, you will ruffle some feathers before you even open your mouth.

To arm you for every conflict and avoid getting caught out, here are some common arguments you may face, and how you can respond. I have had it all thrown at me, and wish I knew then what I know now. I would have had the information to fire back (with compassion, of course)!

THE FOUNDING FALSEHOOD: HUMANS ARE CARNIVORES.

Actually, humans are omnivores, meaning we can eat both plants and meat. However, from an anatomical perspective, we are herbivorous. Humans have short, soft fingernails and small canine teeth. You wouldn't want us hunting and ripping apart flesh in the wild. In contrast, carnivores all have sharp claws and large canine teeth capable of tearing flesh. Like other herbivores and omnivores' teeth, humans' back molars are flat (ideal for grinding fibrous plant foods).

Carnivorous animals swallow their food whole, relying on extremely acidic stomach juices to break down flesh and kill the dangerous bacteria in it, which would otherwise sicken or kill them. Our stomach acids are much weaker in comparison, because strong acids aren't needed to digest chewed fruits and vegetables.

Animals who hunt and eat other animals have short intestinal tracts that allow meat to pass through quickly, before it can rot and cause disease. Our intestinal tracts are much longer than those of carnivores. Longer intestines allow the body more time to break down fiber and absorb nutrients from plant-based foods, but they also make it dangerous for humans to eat a lot of meat. The bacteria in meat have extra time to multiply during the long trip through our gut, increasing the risk of food poisoning and increasing the risk of developing colon cancer.

The biological reality is that we are part of the great apes family. We just need to look at our nearest cousins on earth (like gorillas, orangutans, and chimpanzees): they all eat a plant-based diet.[5]

IT IS NATURAL FOR US TO EAT MEAT BECAUSE HUMANS ARE AT THE TOP OF THE FOOD CHAIN.

In today's industrialized world, we are far removed from any natural food chain or ecosystem. And when we were still in any natural world order or food chain, we were far from the top!

There is a statistical way to work out a species' trophic level—that means its level or rank in a food chain. In 2013, French researchers used food supply data from the UN Food and Agricultural Organization to calculate humans' trophic level. The scale goes from 1 to 5, with 1 being the score of a primary producer (like plants and trees) and 5 being a pure apex predator (animals that only eat meat and have few or no predators of their own, like tigers, sharks, crocodiles, or boa constrictors). They found that humans score 2.21. We are roughly equal to an anchovy or a pig.

Their findings confirm common sense. We are omnivores, we eat a mix of plants and animals, as opposed to top-level predators that only consume meat. Obviously, in modern society, we don't need to worry about a predator eating us or our family. But to truly be at the "top of the food chain" in scientific terms, you have to strictly consume the meat of animals that are predators themselves.[6]

We don't hunt and kill animals with our natural abilities. In fact, most of us would balk at the idea of killing an animal with our bare hands or our teeth. We buy our meat nicely packaged in supermarkets. And there is nothing natural about the way we have bred, genetically modified, and intensively farmed animals we consign to be food in our culture.

THE DESPERATE ONE: PLANTS HAVE FEELINGS TOO.

This seems desperate and hardly worth your time, but it's surprising how much it comes up! Is pulling a carrot from the soil the same as slaughtering a baby calf?

Let's begin with the science—plants do not have a brain, a central nervous system or pain receptors. So, from a scientific point of view, plants do not have the capacity to feel pain.

The confusion comes from the fact that plants are alive. We can watch them grow from a seed into something incredible—but they do this on a cellular level. They react, rather than respond, to their surroundings. Think of it as a doorbell. A doorbell buzzes because it has been pressed, not because it is consciously aware of a finger pressing it.

Animals, on the other hand, respond and react. Anyone who has interacted with a pet knows this. The difference between plants and animals involves sentience. Animals are sentient beings—they have interests, preferences, desires, they use language. It may not be the same language as humans, but that is irrelevant.

From an ethical perspective, we cannot look at the life of a plant in the same way we look at the life of an animal. If I intentionally step on a flower in your garden, you might be mildly annoyed. But if I intentionally kicked your pet, I hope your upset would be quite different!

Bold declarations, such as "vegans murder plants", are thrown out to get a reaction and trigger an argument. Don't rise to the bait. If you feel so inclined, then you could gently remind your antagonist that plants don't feel pain, unlike animals—which is where they should focus their concerns and compassion.

VEGANS DON'T GET ENOUGH PROTEIN.

"Where do you get your protein?" is probably the most common question vegans need to rebut. We're brainwashed from childhood to associate meat with muscles. We're taught that meat and eggs are protein rich, and that's all there is to it. Here you can respond that all the protein from meat-centric diets comes from plants. Cows are only the middleman, and not a very efficient one at that.

The largest study comparing the nutrient intake of meat eaters to plant eaters found that the average person on a plant-based diet doesn't just get enough protein, but 70% more than they need. Ironically, even die-hard meat-eaters get more than half of their protein from plants![7]

Ultimately, you can get more than enough high quality protein on a fully plant-based diet. A peanut butter sandwich or a cup of cooked lentils has the same amount of protein as 3 ounces (90 grams) of beef or 3 eggs![8]

And let's face it—many of the world's largest and strongest animals eat plant-based diets. I've yet to hear anyone ask a horse where it gets its protein. What do the largest and strongest land animals all have in common? The elephant, rhino, and hippopotamus are all vegans and build their massive muscles entirely from plants. And then there is that old expression; strong as an ox—who also happens to be vegan!

MILK BUILDS STRONG BONES.

Q. How do you keep milk fresh?
A. Leave it in the cow.

Humans are the only mammals on the planet that drink the milk of another species. No other animal does this. In evolutionary terms, drinking cow's milk is extremely recent. Humans began domesticating cattle around 10,000 years ago. Before then, only children would drink milk (and it was their mother's milk, not another animal's). When they stopped breastfeeding, they stopped making the digestive enzyme responsible for breaking down and absorbing lactose (the sugar in milk). We have not evolved to drink milk beyond childhood—most of us are lactose intolerant.

The confusion comes because aggressive marketing pushes milk as a healthy drink, while ignoring the mountain of cautionary science. The truth is that the saturated fat, hormones and growth factors in milk are linked to many illnesses, including heart disease, certain cancers, diabetes and obesity. Dairy products also increase the risk of acne, which, while not life-threatening, is emotionally distressing.[9]

With regards to milk being good for bones, studies show that in populations with the highest intake of dairy, like the US, rates of osteoporosis are still incredibly high. This points to the fact that milk does not automatically lead to stronger bones. Calcium does, and you can find calcium elsewhere (see next point).

Basically, we are not baby cows and need milk made for humans. The good news is there are tons of fantastic vegan alternatives to explore, from oat and soy to almond and hazelnut, and even some made from peas and potatoes!

YOU NEED TO EAT DAIRY TO GET ENOUGH CALCIUM.

Calcium comes from the earth. The plants pull it from the soil, cows eat the vegetation, and the calcium passes into their milk. Just like cows get their calcium from plants, we can get calcium directly and more effectively from plants as well. Broccoli, leafy greens, soy, beans, almonds, sesame seeds, amaranth (an ancient grain), berries and figs are all good sources.

What's more, fortified plant milk has a calcium content that is about the same or higher than cow's milk. A glass of whole cow's milk has about 300 milligrams of calcium per cup of milk (around 240 ml). Almond milk contains 451 mg calcium per cup; oat milk contains 350 mg calcium per cup; soy milk contains 450 mg calcium per cup; hemp milk contains 283 mg calcium per cup.[10] So as you can see, you don't need cow's milk to get enough calcium.

IF THE WORLD WENT VEGAN, WE WOULD BE OVERRUN BY ANIMALS!

Another common argument thrown our way is the belief that if we didn't kill all these animals, they would somehow multiply and take over the world. And it's a tricky one to answer and understand.

The main thing here is that the animal farming industry works on a supply and demand basis. You buy meat, and that signals that there is a demand for more of this product. The farming industry is profit driven and would not breed animals if they could not sell them, as this doesn't make economic sense.

We need to be realistic and accept that the world's population will not go vegan overnight, so we will never be faced with a situation where we have 70 billion animals let out to roam free. It will be gradual: as we make more sustainable and vegan choices, meat demand will decline, which means fewer animals being bred for consumption. The populations will adjust—as vegans grow in numbers, the number of farm animals will slowly decline.

IF WE DIDN'T BREED THESE ANIMALS, THEY WOULD GO EXTINCT.
Several things here. The first is that the animals on factory farms would not exist in the wild anyway—they have been genetically manipulated and selectively bred. They are not natural animals. For example, dairy cows are bred to produce ten times more milk than their natural counterparts, and broiler chickens are bred to develop enormous breasts and thighs. They would not survive outside factory farms, so they would need human care. Thankfully, there are many animal sanctuaries, as well as people who dedicate time and money to caring for rescued farm animals.

What's more, with less livestock, we would be able to re-wild and regrow areas razed to make room for CAFOs and feed crops, thereby creating natural habitats for other animal species to flourish.

If you truly care about animal extinction, consider that we are currently in the midst of the largest mass species extinction,[11] and that one of the main drivers for this is animal agriculture. Going vegan is one of the best things you can do to protect the world's biodiversity.

BUT I LOVE THE TASTE OF ANIMAL PRODUCTS!
One of the main justifications for not going more plant-based. Many people profess to love the taste of steaks, chicken, and cheesy pizza. I guess I told myself this as well. But most people don't go vegan just because they don't enjoy the taste of meat.

The important questions to consider are: Do you value taste over life? Are your tastebuds and preferences of more importance than the lives of other sentient beings?

I hope you agree that sensory pleasure is not enough to morally justify any action. Just because it tastes good, that does not justify the torture, nor does it justify the destruction of the Amazon rainforest. What makes it okay is speciesism, the notion that some animals are there to be exploited by humans. This type of reasoning could be applied to any animal—cats, dogs, dolphins, pandas, or elephants. When this justification is used to keep killing some animals, you have to accept it for all animals, including those you love. If this is uncomfortable, perhaps the taste of meat isn't worth it after all.

EATING ANIMALS IS PART OF OUR CULTURE AND TRADITION.
Yes, we have eaten animals for eons. It is ingrained in our culture and tradition. But does it make it morally justifiable?

Why not apply this logic to a human situation to see if it stands up. Not long ago, it was part of culture and tradition to not allow women the right to vote. Only last century, it was cultural and traditional to keep slaves. In some cultures, it is tradition to carry out female genital mutilation. But would we consider these things morally acceptable, just because they are traditional or part of a culture?

Let's apply this logic to animals most of us in the Western world love. China's Yulin dog meat festival takes place every year. It lasts ten days, during which over 10,000 cats and dogs are killed and eaten.[12] Dog eating is a tradition in China, but does that make it okay? What about the Faroe Islands annual whale slaughter, considered an example of traditional aboriginal whaling, where around 800 long-finned pilot whales and some dolphins are killed?[13] It is tradition, but does that justify it?

So the question that follows naturally is, if tradition does not morally justify the slaughter of animals we love (dogs, cats, dolphins, etc.), then how does it morally justify our killing of cows, pigs, and chickens? The answer is simple.

It doesn't.

WHY AREN'T VEGANS FOCUSING ON HUMAN RIGHTS INSTEAD?

With so many human rights issues, why are vegans so bothered about animals? Shouldn't they focus on human problems instead? This is a common criticism thrown at vegans.

Firstly, being vegan does not preclude you from being passionate about other issues facing our world. You can be vegan and a humanitarian activist. The two aren't mutually exclusive. Also, ranking injustices and arguing about which one should be solved first doesn't get us anywhere. Should it be homelessness? Should it be the war in Syria? Should it be worker exploitation? Should it be childhood poverty? Should it be famine? While we're debating what to focus on, nothing changes.

You can be vegan and fight for all sorts of other causes. Just because you choose to eat plants doesn't mean you ignore all the other problems going on in the world.

What's more, industrial animal farming is not just an animal welfare issue. It is a human rights issue because the majority of people working in the industry are exploited, poorly paid, and work in atrocious conditions that destroy their physical and mental health. It's a global human rights issue because the grain fed to livestock could feed the millions of people currently going hungry. Human rights are an intrinsic part of going vegan.

BUT ISN'T ORGANIC OR ETHICALLY SOURCED MEAT OKAY?

You must have heard something like the following: "I really care about animal welfare, so I only buy humane and free range products, so the animals have lived a good life and felt no pain."

Labels like Red Tractor Approved, RSPCA Approved, Humanely Slaughtered, High-Welfare, and Free-range don't mean much. They don't represent any improvement for the animals. Taking a hen out of a cage and putting it into an overcrowded barn doesn't actually improve its welfare. These labels are simply there to ease the consumer's conscience. Animals are still being exploited, are still suffering, are still scared, and are still slaughtered on a factory line with little consideration for whether or not they want to die.

Humane slaughter is an oxymoron. It is not possible. Being humane means having and showing compassion and benevolence. Can you compassionately, benevolently, humanely take the life of an animal that does not want to die? The only way to humanely slaughter animals is...to not slaughter them. The only happy animals are those who get to live out their lives in freedom—not confined to cages and airless sheds, not standing in their own feces, not castrated, tagged, mutilated and pumped full of medications.

Yes, improving the treatment of these animals is better than not doing anything. But the impact these measures can have is tiny, because at the end of the day, the animal still has to suffer and die. There is no right way to do the wrong thing.

Let's take free-range as an example. It is simply a marketing ploy. We believe free-range means that the hens that produce the eggs live a happy, fulfilled life. This is a lie. These hens are still debeaked, the male chicks are still killed at birth, the sheds are still so overcrowded that most of these free range hens will not experience sunlight or the outside world, and they will still be sent to slaughter once they are no longer laying enough eggs.[14] Legal requirements for free range eggs are nine hens per square meter, one drinker per ten birds, and ten centimeters of feeder space.[15] How spacious and airy does that sound to you?

Animals don't want to be free-range, they want to be free. Free to live their life without human-inflicted suffering. The thing is, no matter how "good" animals' lives have been, the moment we exploit them for something that is not ours, the moment we take them to the slaughterhouse, we are abusing them. There is no way to morally justify this when we can obtain all the nutrients we need from plants.

VEGANS ARE MALNOURISHED.

This is another common "concern" we may receive from friends and family. If it's not about protein, then it's about B12 and Omega-3. The first question that comes up for me when asked about this is: do you ask everyone about their protein/B12/Omega-3? Given the high occurrence of chronic disease due to the standard Western diet,[16] it would make more sense to target people who eat meat and junk foods with your concern.

Actually, vegan diets are perfectly adequate on all levels. This is not an opinion, but a fact supported by the Canadian Dietetics Association, Dietitians of Canada, the British Dietetic Association[17] and the American Dietetic Association.[18]

According to these recognized and respected institutions, "Well planned vegan and other types of vegetarian diets are appropriate for all stages of the life cycle, including during pregnancy, lactation, infancy, childhood and adolescence." They go on to say that plant-based diets offer "a number of nutritional benefits, including lower levels of saturated fats, cholesterol, and animal protein, as well as higher levels of carbohydrates, fiber, magnesium, potassium, folate, and antioxidants such as vitamins C and E and phytochemicals."[19]

If a plant-based diet was such a problem for nourishment, then why are so many elite athletes changing to plant-based rather than the high meat/high protein diets of days gone by? And when we are talking about elite athletes, we mean it—these are the ultramarathon runners, world-class athletes and body-builders who employ the top nutritionists to squeeze out every last ounce of energy to improve their game.

VEGANS DON'T GET ENOUGH VITAMIN B12

Yes, it is difficult to get on a vegan diet, but vegans are not alone in being at risk of vitamin B12 deficiency. Some people lack the intrinsic factor (a protein made by the cells of the digestive tract) necessary to absorb B12. People with anemia or who take proton pump inhibitors (for stomach acid) also struggle to absorb B12.[20]

According to the National Institute of Health, up to 40% of the Western population has low or marginal vitamin B12 status.[21] This could be because the B12 naturally present in animal foods is difficult to absorb. For this reason, the Institute of Medicine advises the intake of foods (cereals, plant milks, etc.) that have been fortified with B12. Another option is to take a high-quality B12 supplement.

As for Omega-3, as we explored in the Health section of the Driving Forces chapter, fish get their Omega-3 from algae, and vegans can too. There are plenty of algae-based Omega-3 options. You can also obtain this nutrient from plant foods such as walnuts, hemp seeds, flax seeds, chia seeds, edamame beans, and kidney beans.

Aside from B12, there is no nutrient that you cannot obtain from plants. By eating a wide variety of plant foods, you will give your body everything it needs to thrive and live a long, healthy life.

There is a quiet confidence that comes with living your best life in line with your values. But you still need to be ready to be confronted by people who have an opinion about your dietary choices. Be ready to stand your ground. But do so with kindness, grace and tolerance. The best way to respond to skepticism is simply to state your truth, accepting that the person in front of you may disagree.

I believe that the best thing you can do is lead by example. Compassion is at the core of veganism, so remember to be compassionate to people who are at a different point on the spectrum.

This is how *REBEL VEGANS* can support the movement and help save the world. Not by fighting or arguing, but by being open, authentic, compassionate, and fabulous!

12

FINAL THOUGHTS

VIVA LA REVOLUTION

*'If they don't give you a seat at the table,
bring a folding chair.'*
**Shirley Chisholm, First Black congresswoman (1968)
and presidential nominee (1972)**

There comes a time when we need to take an honest look at life. That is what you've done by reading this book—you've confronted the truth behind our traditional diet. It can be an uncomfortable truth but one we ignore at our peril.

We all grew up within the dominant belief system where eating meat is promoted as natural, and part of who we are, but it is killing us. As we have seen in the driving forces chapters, eating meat is one of the worst things that you can do for your own wellbeing as well as that of society, animals, and the planet.

Today's industrialized meat industry is unimaginably cruel to animals, undeniably destructive to our planet, and shockingly exploitative of its workforce. It has gifted us pandemic after pandemic and is in part responsible for the chronic diseases that plague our world. The mounting evidence is unequivocal, undeniable, and requires us all to act. We all have a role in creating this brave new world and it needs us to take our heads out of the sand.

We have a tiny window of opportunity left to us if we want to turn things around. However, no solution is complete without us moving further along the spectrum towards a plant-based diet. No amount of shorter showers or solar panels will save our world if we keep alone if the industry grows, as predicted. By coming on this journey, you are part of the solution.

As I travel the world, spreading the good word, I realize that vegan values are all our values. We're more alike than different. We all care about animals, justice, the environment, and our health. We all want the same things. And we are in this together.

You are a *REBEL VEGAN*, and you are part of the solution. Wherever you are on the spectrum, as you move towards a more plant-based life, you are sending a strong message: the world is changing, and you are changing with it.

This book was always about celebrating what's great about food, and not about restricting yourself. Returning to my true state of compassion and alignment has been the most rewarding adventure of my life. Veganism is the ultimate destination of one of life's greatest journeys.

Thank you for joining the rebellion, making this brave choice, being on the right side of history, and a force for good. It takes determination and strength to stand in the face of the dominant belief system and challenge the conditioning of our society. But with your help, *REBEL VEGANS* will keep flying the flag until the rest of the world catches up.

We are starting a revolution,

one meal at a time!

13

RESOURCES

In my years of veganism and travel, I have collected a treasure trove of resources to help me along my way. I've done my best to share this knowledge and information with you in my Rebel Vegan series. To help you quickly access this information while on the go, I have compiled all of the resources mentioned in this guide into one compact resource section. Feel free to dogear these pages and references when needed in your life and adventures.

WEBSITES
Save these websites to your Favorites Bar before preparing your next vegan vacation. These resources will make the planning process considerably easier.

- **Plant Based Health Online:** The top plant-based doctors in the UK offering healthcare and lifestyle advice to overcome chronic illnesses and certain cancers. *PlantBasedHealthOnline.com*

- **HappyCow:** This website is helpful for finding vegan restaurants around the world. It is user-sourced, so you can add or update restaurants, as well as read customer reviews. Bonus, this website comes in app form too. *HappyCow.net*

- **VegVisits:** The Airbnb for vegans. Book unique homestays and accommodations with locals in over 80 countries. *VegVisits.com*

- **Vegan Meetups, Couchsurfing, and Traveling:** A Facebook community with 7,000 members. Vegan gatherings and open Couchsurfing opportunities are listed here. Members also discuss travel experiences and questions. You have to request membership for this group. *facebook.com/groups/974772789309783*

- **Barnivore:** A searchable directory of wines, beers, and liquors denoting which are vegan-friendly. *barnivore.com*

- **Vegan Travel Facebook Group:** The group currently has over 35,000 members. The content discusses all things vegan related, and many members are more than happy to answer your questions. *facebook.com/groups/vegantravel*

- **Vegan Travel:** Virtual vegan community with reviews, blog posts, videos, and more for planning your vegan trips. *VeganTravel.com*

- **Foundation for Intentional Community:** Want to live with other vegans? Interested in growing your own food? How about popping in for a weekend visit? Use this website to access a global directory of intentional communities. The advanced search option lets users narrow the search to vegetarian and/or vegan communities. *ic.org*

- **Food Labels Exposed:** Use this website put together by A Greener World to help you navigate the confusing world of food labels. *aGreenerWorld.org/wp-content/uploads/2015/03/AGW-Food-Labels-Exposed-2017-EMAIL-SCREEN-8-31-2017.pdf*

- **Animal Welfare's Consumer's Guide:** The Animal Welfare Institute has put together a listing of all food labels and what they mean, explaining which are legal terms and which are made up by the food companies. *awiOnline.org/content/consumers-guide-food-labels-and-animal-welfare*

- **Vegan Calculator:** Ever wished you could measure the impact you've made in your vegan or vegetarian journey? Now you can. Measure your impact at: *VeganCalculator.com*

- **Book Different:** This website rates hotels in terms of their eco-friendliness. *BookDifferent.com*

APPS

Download these apps on your phone ASAP! These resources will help you with just about everything - booking a hotel room, scoring a yummy vegan meal, communicating in a foreign language, and more.

- **Vegan Passport:** This is a digital food card available in various languages to help you explain your dietary preferences. The passport explains in detail which ingredients vegans do and don't eat in 78 different languages.

- **Google Translate:** You can speak or type words and phrases to be translated into over 100 languages. You can even point your camera at a block of text and have it translated for you in real-time. Be sure to download the language pack for the specific language you need, so that the app can be used offline as well.

- **AirVegan:** Use this app when heading to the airport. AirVegan shows how vegan-friendly an airport is. It lists all places that offer vegan options, and even tells you where they are located. Some of you may have encountered this app back when they only supported airports in the United States. Good news - the app went international with its listings back in 2018.

- **Food Monster:** This app provides the user with a database containing over 8,000 vegan recipes. While it isn't travel-related, it can aid you in your travels by providing quick and budget-friendly meals when you select the filters 'Less Than Five Ingredients' or 'Quick Meals'.

- **VeganXpress:** This app only works for travel in the US. It lists all vegan menu choices at 150 chain restaurants throughout the US. The database goes into great detail about all the possible vegan options. It also includes a food guide for supermarkets, and another guide for various alcoholic drinks.

- **V-Cards:** Vegan Abroad: V-cards, vegan cards in this case, are translation cards to help you order food abroad. This is a similar concept to the food cards offered up in the Hot Spots chapter of this guide, only they offer translations in over 100 languages on demand.

- **Veganagogo:** This is another translation app - because you can never have too many. Users choose from a list of pre-written questions and statements, making it easier to use than Google Translate in some scenarios.

- **Foodsaurus:** Standing in the grocery aisle at a foreign market completely unsure of what the ingredient list on the pre-made boxed meal lists? Whip out your phone and scan the ingredient list with Foodsaurus, and the app will translate the label to your language of choice.

- **Veggly:** Can't imagine dating an omnivore? Looking for a romantic partner that can hold you accountable in your vegan journey? Check out Veggly, a vegan dating app currently available in 181 countries.

- **Vegan Check:** This app double checks that products are entirely vegan before purchasing. It also includes services such as tattoo studios and salons.

- **Vegan Pocket:** Vegan Pocket scans barcodes to check if the product is vegan. No more reading confusing food labels! Just scan, and done.

- **abillion | Impact made easy:** This app lets you search for vegan brands and products near you, wherever you are around the world. After finding a vegan product on the app, you can even read customer reviews.

VOLUNTEERING

Want to get involved? Use these websites to find volunteer opportunities in the vegan community.

- **WWOOF:** Worldwide opportunities to volunteer on organic farms. Typically, room and board are offered in exchange. You must create an account for each country you would like to search for hosts in, and a subscription fee is required. *wwoof.net*

- **WorkAway:** Worldwide opportunities to volunteer at organic and non-organic farms, homesteads, communities, non-profit organizations, and more. Room and board are typically offered in exchange. Sometimes hosts offer an hourly wage in addition to this. A small subscription fee is required. *WorkAway.info*

- **HelpX:** HelpX is the same concept as WorkAway (above), without the opportunity for an hourly wage. Room and board are usually offered, and a small subscription fee is required. *helpx.net*

- **Voluntouring:** This blog keeps an up-to-date listing of organizations looking for volunteers. The listing has a tab for listings that strictly adhere to vegan principles. *voluntouring.org*

- **International Volunteering:** Facebook group listing international vegan-based volunteer opportunities. *facebook.com/groups/217244375670902*

- **Grassroots Volunteering:** Database of international grassroots volunteer experiences. Search the site for vegan-centered opportunities, or contact hosts to see if vegans can be accommodated. *GrassRootsVolunteering.org*

- **WorldPackers:** Volunteer experiences and programs for travelers in over 100 countries. *WorldPackers.com*

VEGAN TOURS

These vegan tour guides and agencies take the work and planning out of your adventure, leaving nothing but fun and delicious plant-based food for you. Each has detailed websites listing all of their services and destinations! Even if you don't plan on booking with an agency, they are worth looking at for inspiration and ideas.

P.S. These are tour groups offering international opportunities. If you already have a destination in mind, do a quick Google search for vegan tour guides there. I bet you'll find even more resources!

- **Vegan Food Tours:** European Vegan City Tours.
  VeganFoodTours.com
- **Vegan Adventure Tours:** Specialising in epic tours through Latin American and UK micro tours.
  VeganAdventureHolidays.com
- **Intrepid Travel:** International tour company does several vegan tours annually.
  IntrepidTravel.com/vegan-food-adventures
- **The Nomadic Vegan:** Website for Vegan Tours, Vegan Cruise, and Vegan-friendly tour operators.
  TheNomadicVegan.com/vegan-tours

FESTS AND EVENTS

A great way to have fun and immerse in the vegan culture while traveling is to attend a festival or event. Below I list a number of resources for finding events in several destinations. This list is not exhaustive! Reference it, and then do further research to find even more fun items to add to your travel calendar.

- **Vegan Festivals Directory:** *vegan.com/blog/festivals*
- **VegEvents International:** *VegEvents.com*
- **International Listing:** *vegan.com/blog/festivals*
- **Vegan Society International Listings:** *VeganSociety.com/ whats-new/events*
- **HappyCow International Listings:** *HappyCow.net/events*
- **UK Vegan Events:** VeganEventsUK.co.uk
- **USA Vegan Events:** AmericanVegan.org/vegfests
- **Australia Vegan Events:** VeganAustralia.org.au/events

FILMS:

- Cowspiracy (Netflix)
- Seaspiracy (Netflix)
- Earthlings (Free stream on http://www.nationearth.com/)
- The Game Changers (Netflix)
- What The Health (YouTube)
- Forks Over Knives (YouTube)
- The End of Meat (YouTube)
- Meat Me Halfway (YouTube/ Amazon Prime)
- Eating Our Way to Extinction (Amazon Prime)
- The Invisible Vegan (Amazon Prime)
- The Animal People (Amazon Prime)
- A Prayer for Compassion (Amazon Prime)
- My Octopus Teacher (Netflix)
- Okja (Netflix)

My Top Pic: Babe / Babe: Pig in the City (Amazon or Netflix)

BOOKS

Classic Reads:

- **Vegetable Diet: As Sanctioned by Medical Men, and by Experience in All Ages (1838) by William A Alcott:** The world's first book to advocate a vegetarian diet! It's been reprinted by The American Antiquarian Cookbook Collection and still in print today.

- **Diet for a Small Planet (1971) by Frances Moore Lappe:** A groundbreaking book arguing that world hunger is caused by the meat industry. It was the first time that meat was shown to be unhealthy and leading to global poverty.

- **Animal Liberation (1975) by Peter Singer:** This book is widely considered the founding philosophical statement of its ideas within the animal liberation movement. Singer claimed that industrial farming is responsible for more pain and misery than all the wars of history put together.

- **Main Street Vegan: Everything You Need to Know to Eat Healthfully and Live Compassionately in the Real World (2012) by Victoria Moran:** Holistic health practitioner Victoria Moran offers a complete guide to making this dietary and lifestyle shift with an emphasis on practical "baby steps," proving that you don't have to have a personal chef or lifestyle coach on speed dial to experience the physical and spiritual benefits of being a vegan.

- **The China study: The Most Comprehensive Study of Nutrition Ever Conducted and the Startling Implications for Diet, Weight Loss and Long-Term Health (2004) by T. Colin Cambell:** This novel takes the reader through a twenty-year study which looked at mortality rates from cancer and other chronic diseases from 1973 to 1975 in 65 counties in China. The China Study examines the link between the consumption of animal products (including dairy) and chronic illnesses such as coronary heart disease, diabetes, breast cancer, prostate cancer, and bowel cancer.

Modern Reads:

- **Why We Love Dogs, Eat Pigs, and Wear Cows by Melanie Joy:** The social psychologist who coined the word and hidden belief system of "carnism." (Her YouTube channel is good as well).

- **Beyond Beliefs: A Guide to Improving Relationships and Communication for Vegans, Vegetarians, and Meat Eaters by Melanie Joy, PhD:** This book is recommended for anyone living with or in close relationships with non-vegans.

- **We Are the Weather: Saving the Planet Begins at Breakfast by Jonathon Safran Foer:** This book explains how collective human action is the only way to save the planet, and as the title suggests, this begins with what is on our plates.

- **Eating Animals by Jonathon Safran Foer:** Part memoir, part investigative report. This book is a moral examination of vegetarianism, farming, and the food we eat.

- **Sex Robots & Vegan Meat: Adventures at the Frontier of Birth, Food, Sex, and Death by Jenny Kleeman:** This novel is an investigation into the forces driving innovation in the core areas of human experience.

- **Some We Love, Some We Eat, Some We Hate: Why It's So Hard to Think Straight About Animals by Hal Herzog:** A scientist in the field of anthrozoology offers a controversial exploration of the psychology behind the ways we think, feel, and behave towards animals.

***All restaurants, applications, websites, and other resources are up to date as of the time of publishing.

Times are turbulent, and therefore dynamic. Always double check to ensure organizations are still in operation.

14

APPENDICES

APPENDIX 1 - LABELS EXPLAINED

Crate-free (pork)
This claim is not defined by the USDA. It indicates the animal was not housed in a gestation crate (used to confine sows during pregnancy) or a farrowing crate (used to confine sows from just before birth until the piglets are weaned). Some producers use the claim to signify no gestation crates only, while still using farrowing crates. This also does not tell the buyer anything about how the pigs were treated.

Ethically raised / Responsibly raised / Thoughtfully raised
None of these claims are defined by the USDA, and there is no third-party certification program to check these claims. The only thing the producer must do is explain what they mean by the claim that animals were "thoughtfully" raised. If you see this on a label, consider it a marketing tactic with no relevance to animal welfare.

Halal
The US Humane Methods of Slaughter Act exempts animals killed for religious purposes from the requirement that they be stunned (to make them insensitive to pain), before shackling, hoisting and cutting. This means Halal products come from animals slaughtered without being stunned. In other words, animals are fully conscious of what is happening to them.

Kosher
As with Halal products, kosher meats and poultry are typically produced from animals that have not been made insensitive to pain prior to slaughter.

Natural
This claim can be used on eggs and dairy, but the USDA definition only applies to meat and poultry. The claim "natural" can be used on products that have been minimally processed and are free from artificial ingredients or added colors. An explanation must accompany the claim for the use of the term. Unless stated, "natural" does not mean that no antibiotics or hormones were given to the animal. The claim has no relevance to how the animals were raised.

Naturally raised
This claim indicates the product has come from animals that have not been given antibiotics or hormones, and were fed a vegetarian diet. However, this does not require any improvement to living conditions, such as access to pasture or range

No added hormones / No hormones administered
The US government prohibits the use of hormones for poultry, veal, eggs, bison and pork. A claim of "No added hormones" should come with a statement to say the administration of hormones is prohibited by federal regulation. This has no relevance to how animals are raised and slaughtered. It should be considered purely a marketing ploy.

Omega-3-enriched
This just means that Omega-3 (in the form of flaxseed, algae or fish oil) was added to feed given to the hens that produced those eggs. This claim bears no relevance to animal welfare.

United Egg Producers (UEP) certified
This certification program was developed by and for the egg industry, and is therefore not independent. The standards allow hens to be crowded in tiny cages for their entire lives, beak trimming without pain-relief, and no access to pasture, fresh air or sunlight.

USDA Process Verified
The USDA offers this "Process Verified Program" seal as a marketing tool to producers. Producers can submit their own standards for consideration, and the USDA audits to verify that the company is following the standards they set themselves. This means terms like "humanely handled" and "animal care" vary widely between producers, but are all eligible to receive the USDA Process Verified certificate. Many of these products come from factory-farmed animals, where animal welfare is not a priority.

Vegetarian fed
Putting aside the fact it's worrying that cattle should be fed anything other than plants, being herbivores, this claim only means that the animal feed used is free from animal-derived by-products. It has no relevance to how the animal was raised or slaughtered.

APPENDIX 2 - MEAT MOTIVATORS IN ADVERTISING

ALPHA MALE COMPLEX

Fear: Being a weakling, being called a "beta" man (as opposed to alpha).

Desire: Strength, muscles, masculinity.

Ah, that old, reassuring status quo of the man as a big beefy meathead who slaps down a carcass on the table for his cavewoman concubine to cook. Never mind if that's not really how it went down, men still want to feel like men - preferably alpha, big and strong. And you can't get big and strong on beans, can you? (vegan athletes prove differently, but let's ignore that for now). More meat equals more muscle! Somewhere in the back of our mind, we still believe if we eat three chickens a day and egg smoothies, we'll get big like Arnie or Stallone.

GOOD MOTHER COMPLEX

Fear: Not doing right by your baby.

Desire: To give your baby everything they need.

Mothers just want the best for their children. And so here come those soothing, pastel-shaded adverts that, in a soft voice, tell us baby formula contains everything your baby needs for health. The dairy industry knows we want to be good parents, and capitalizes on it. Unfortunately, baby formula is not the best for your baby, however many images of reassuring motherhood are plastered on our screens. Cow's milk is for baby cows. Not for baby humans.

HEALTHY AGEING (FOR WOMEN)

Fear: Bones turning to dust post-menopause.

Desire: Staying youthful and agile as long as possible.

The myth that milk protects us from osteoporosis is still spread as if rooted in solid science. This does not explain why in countries with the highest intake of dairy, like the USA, rates of osteoporosis remain incredibly high. If dairy really protected against brittle bones, how is it that while dairy consumption has increased year after year (going from 32.1 pounds (14.5 kilos) of cheese consumed per year per person in 2000 to 40.4 pounds (18.33 kilos) of cheese per year per person in 2019), osteoporosis rates have also gone up? (from 33.6 million people in 2002 to 47.5 million people in 2020)

Something is not quite aligning.[1]

TRADITION AND BELONGING

Fear: The loss of familiar, secure traditions.

Desire: To belong.

Meat is part of our lives, and the industry won't let us forget it. Whether it's the comfort of a bacon sandwich in the morning, the joy of a sizzling summer barbecue, the quintessential greasy kebab after a night out, the celebratory roast turkey at Christmas or Thanksgiving, rare are the seasonal adverts that don't feature some type of animal product. This keeps meat firmly in our culture, even though our health and that of the planet is calling for us to release these old habits and forge new ones.

APPENDIX 3 - WHAT DO FACTORY-FARMED ANIMALS EAT?

Animal feed includes the rendered remains of animals. This means things like meat and bone meal, poultry by-product meal, dried animal blood, feather meal, hydrolysed leather meal, eggshell meal, hydrolysed whole poultry, hydrolysed hair, unborn calf carcasses, animal digest, bone marrow, and animal plasma.

Rendering is an industrial process in which animal carcasses, body parts and waste are ground up, heated, and further processed to produce various products, including animal feed.

Here is a short sample of some of the ingredients used in animal feed:

1. **Ingredients from slaughtered food-producing animals:** Around a third of the weight of an animal is not used directly for human consumption. Fat trim, viscera, blood, bones, feathers and hide is collected and processed by the rendering industry.

2. **Ingredients from animals that have died other than by slaughter:** This includes animals that were too ill to reach the slaughterhouse, as well as roadkill, euthanized companion animals (cats and dogs) and other euthanized animals.

3. **4-D animals (dead, dying, diseased or disabled):** 4-D animals are sold to salvagers for use as animal feed.

4. **Animal waste:** Animal waste such as dried cow manure, dried poultry waste, dried poultry litter and dried swine waste. The issue is that poultry litter can contain poultry feed that has spilled onto the litter. Poultry feed contains bovine meat. So we still have a situation where cows can be given feed that contains cow remains. This is what originally gave rise to mad cow disease (BSE).

5. **Dairy products:** Skimmed milk, buttermilk, chocolate milk, whey products, cheese rinds and dried milk protein also make it into animal feed.

6. **Polyethylene:** Plastic pellets are used to replace roughage in feedlot rations for finishing slaughter cattle. It is used at 0.5 pounds (0.23 kilos) per head for six days.

7. **Hazardous waste:** For example, zinc oxide from emission control dust from electric arc furnaces (which is listed as hazardous waste) is authorized to be used as a nutritional feed supplement for animals.

8. **Other additives:** such as artificial sweeteners, colour additives and extracts (used to give chicken skin and eggs a yellow colour) and formaldehyde (used to keep feed free from salmonella for 21 days).

And all this doesn't even take into consideration the amount of drugs and hormones pumped into the animals to keep them the right size and growing at an accelerated rate to maximize profits. Nor have we touched on the vast volume of antibiotics required to keep them alive long enough to even reach slaughter. The potential for antibiotic resistance to grow is enormous as a ludicrous 80%[2] of all antibiotics in the world are used in animal agriculture, not for treating humans.

Locked up, crammed in, abused, and fed a diet a million miles from their natural one. Is there any part of these animals' lives that is not traumatized by the industrial farming industry?

APPENDIX 4 - COMMON PATHOGENS IN MEAT & DAIRY

SALMONELLA:

The salmonella bacteria are present in the digestive tract. Salmonella food poisoning is caused by eating foods contaminated by feces. According to a study published in the journal Clinical Microbiology and Infection, the main sources of salmonella infections in humans are meat products, and in particular poultry meat.[1]

This is not surprising given the conditions in which the animals are kept, and because the speed of slaughter lines does not allow enough time for the animals to be properly eviscerated. As a result, much of the meat is contaminated with salmonella.

Salmonella causes 93.8 million illnesses and 155,000 deaths worldwide every year. [reference: S.E. Majowicz, J. Musto, E. Scallan, F.J. Angulo, M. Kirk, S.J. O'Brien, et al. The global burden of nontyphoidal Salmonella gastroenteritis, Clin Infect Dis, 50 (2010), pp. 882-8890).

CAMPYLOBACTER:

One of four key global causes of diarrheal diseases worldwide, and the most common bacterial cause of human gastroenteritis. According to the World Health Organization, 1 in 10 people fall ill with campylobacter every year, causing a loss of 33 million healthy life years.[2]

In the UK, 80% of campylobacter infections are due to contaminated poultry.[3] In the USA, it causes an estimated 1.5 million illnesses every year.[4]

Campylobacter is found in the guts and feces of warm-blooded animals. Here again, contamination happens because animals live in their own waste for months and because industrial slaughterhouses and meat packing plants do not allow for proper food safety protocols.[5]

STAPHYLOCOCCUS AUREUS:

This pathogen is one of the major food-borne pathogens in the world. Staphylococcus aureus bacteria is found naturally on the skin, hair and mucosal lining of humans and animals. It is generally a commensal part of the microbiome (commensal means there is a mutually beneficial relationship between host and bacteria), however it can also become an opportunistic pathogen and is a common cause of skin infections, pneumonia and food poisoning.[6]

Staphylococcus aureus can adapt to its environment and quickly become resistant to drugs. One example is MRSA (methicillin-resistant S. aureus), which is now a worldwide problem and was listed by the World Health Organization as one of the 12 families of bacteria that pose the greatest threat to human health.[7]

MRSA strains have been found in pigs, cattle and poultry, as well as raw meat.

A study published in the journal Clinical Infectious Diseases found that 47% of all meat and poultry samples in the USA were contaminated with staphylococcus aureus, and half of those were resistant to three classes of antibiotics. [reference: The Translational Genomics Research Institute. (2011, April 15). US meat and poultry is widely contaminated with drug-resistant Staph bacteria, study finds. ScienceDaily.[8]

Drug resistant salmonella, drug-resistant campylobacter, and drug-resistant staphylococcus are all listed on the CDC's Antibiotic Resistance Threats in the United States, 2019 report.[9]

E. COLI:

E. Coli bacteria is found in the stomach, intestines and feces of warm-blooded animals. Shiva toxin-producing E. Coli (STEC) causes severe foodborne disease, and the primary cause of STEC outbreaks are ground meat products, raw milk, and fecal contamination of vegetables.[10]

During the slaughtering and butchering process, E. Coli gets on the surface of the meat or can become incorporated into meat products, like minced beef. This again is due to fast-moving slaughter lines. Some strains of E. Coli can cause diarrhea, bloody diarrhea, vomiting, stomach pain, cramps, as well as kidney failure.

STEC infection was the third most reported zoonosis in humans between 2015 and 2019, according to the European Centre for Disease Prevention and Control.[11]

ACKNOWLEDGMENTS

This book has been a labor of love borne out of the isolation of seemingly endless lockdowns. I was alone and often angry while researching and writing Rebel Vegan Life. But I was never bored.

I was blessed to have had my own virtual mastermind groups to comfort, challenge, and cajole throughout this new and turbulent process. Even when one book became three, the support and belief never wavered. There were moments I wanted to give up, but the faith invested in me kept me going through the long winter. (And I couldn't bear to let any of you down!)

My family taught me the value of hard work, community, and love. I was always a rebel, but you gave me acceptance and taught me to fight for what's right. Wherever I wander, you are my home.

Many beautiful friends had a massive impact on me and these books. Thank you, Emma, for being my rock at every twist and turn. This book could never have happened without your support, advice, and belief in me. Thank you, Lee, for school night brainstorming and coming up with my title. Rachel always gave direct feedback, corrected my grammar, and I love you for it. Yodé for making me laugh at myself and Osaro for mixing the drinks. Sophia would have given me the (car boot) shirt off her back, but instead gave me invaluable advice and even her brand. You are my dream team of rebels, and I love you all.

Writing this book involved many specialists in helping translate some of my medical and scientific research. Special thanks to my nutritionist Mel for patiently explaining all the health implications and becoming a friend in the process.

To my excellent editor, Gareth, thank you for your precision, perspective, and turning vegan. I am not easy to edit, but you did so with patience and kindness. While I turned you vegan, you guided this ship into port. Maybe a fair tradeoff, but I still feel the lucky one.

Elaine, my copywriter, was like a blast of positivity and fun exactly when I needed that boost. Thank you for polishing my words, giving me direction, and making me look good.

I am incredibly grateful to my talented design team: Marco, for designing my logo, Jelena for bringing my book cover concept to life, and my neighbor Cathy for the fantastic illustrations that bring the book alive.

My assistant Ruth has been my loyal cheerleader despite my endless messages and insecurities. You deserve a raise!

And ultimately, thank you, dear reader, for trusting the efforts of this labor of love, for taking this journey and joining this movement for justice and compassion for our planet and all its inhabitants.

I celebrate your courage in building a brave new world.

ABOUT THE AUTHOR

TODD SINCLAIR is the author of the *REBEL VEGAN LIFE* series.

A passionate travel expert, activist, podcaster, writer & speaker for the vegan cause, Todd currently lives his best *REBEL VEGAN LIFE* based in London.

If not writing in his favorite city, you can find him exploring the world—perfecting his cooking in Southeast Asia, trekking volcanoes, or scuba diving, all while promoting plant-based living and putting veganism on the map.

Find out more about *REBEL VEGAN* at the website
RebelVeganLife.com

Or on Social Media

facebook.com/RebelVeganLife
instagram.com/RebelVeganLife

ALSO BY TODD SINCLAIR

REBEL VEGAN LIFE:
A Radical Take on Veganism for a Brave New World

REBEL VEGAN LIFE:
An Essential Plant-Based Nutrition
& Survival Guide for Beginners

REBEL VEGAN LIFE:
The Ultimate Travel Guide for
Plant-Based Adventures in a Brave New World

REFERENCE NOTES

NOT ANOTHER VEGAN
1   https://www.vegansociety.com/
2   https://www.bmj.com/content/369/bmj.m2237

01 RECLAIMING OUR HISTORY
1   https://www.nationalgeographic.com/foodfeatures/evolution-of-diet/
2   https://www.nationalgeographic.com/foodfeatures/evolution-of-diet/
3   https://www.tandfonline.com/doi/abs/10.1080/1751696X.2021.1903177
4   https://www.nationalgeographic.com/foodfeatures/evolution-of-diet/
5   https://www.nytimes.com/2002/02/26/science/when-humans-became-human.html
6   https://www.nytimes.com/2002/02/26/science/when-humans-became-human.html
7   https://www.nationalgeographic.com/science/article/chimps-humans-96-percent-the-same-gene-study-finds
8   https://blogs.scientificamerican.com/guest-blog/human-ancestors-were-nearly-all-vegetarians/
9   http://www.perseus.tufts.edu/hopper/text?doc=urn:cts:greekLit:tlg0007.tlg131.perseus-eng1:5
10 https://www.nationalgeographic.com/foodfeatures/evolution-of-diet/
11 https://www.nationalgeographic.com/foodfeatures/evolution-of-diet/
12 https://www.youtube.com/watch?v=i-dVlMdY-JQ
13 https://www.huffpost.com/entry/are-buddhists-vegetarians_b_59c7c589e4b0f2df5e83af35
14 https://www.bbc.co.uk/religion/religions/christianity/christianethics/animals_1.shtml
15 https://www.milliondollarvegan.com/what-does-the-bible-say-about-veganism/
16 https://www.milliondollarvegan.com/what-does-the-bible-say-about-veganism/
17 https://biblehub.com/kjv/mark/16.htm
18 https://tamidnyc.org/113-tzar-baal-hachahim-caring-animals-2/
19 http://www.touregypt.net/featurestories/animalgods.htm
20 https://www.thoughtco.com/top-special-animals-in-greek-mythology-118586
21 https://www.independent.co.uk/life-style/who-were-the-world-s-very-earliest-vegans-a7668831.html
22 https://www.britannica.com/explore/savingearth/the-hidden-history-of-greco-roman-vegetarianism
23 https://www.ancient.eu/Pythagoras/
24 https://en.wikipedia.org/wiki/Apollonius_of_Tyana#cite_note-18
25 https://bulletin.hds.harvard.edu/the-secular-religion-of-plotinus/
26 http://www.perseus.tufts.edu/hopper/text?doc=urn:cts:greekLit:tlg0007.tlg131.perseus-eng1:5
27 https://en.wikipedia.org/wiki/Akhenaten
28 https://en.wikipedia.org/wiki/Emperor_Tenmu#Politics
29 https://fromgreens.com/galleryphoto/abraham-lincoln-quotes/
30 http://www.humanedecisions.com/benjamin-franklin-said-eating-flesh-is-unprovoked-murder/
31 https://vegsoc.org/about-us/world-history-of-vegetarianism/
32 https://en.wikipedia.org/wiki/George_Cheyne_(physician)#Vegetarianism
33 https://www.oxfordscholarlyeditions.com/view/10.1093/actrade/9780198205166.book.1/actrade-9780198205166-work-1
34 https://www.bl.uk/collection-items/p-b-shelleys-a-vindication-of-the-natural-diet
35 https://en.wikiquote.org/wiki/Donald_Watson
36 https://vegsoc.org/about-us/world-history-of-vegetarianism/
37 Vegetarian Messenger, 1923, 77, cited in Leneman, 221. And
    https://www.vegansociety.com/sites/default/files/uploads/Ripened%20by%20human%20determination.pdf
38 Vegetarian Messenger, 1935, 235 cited in Leneman, 221. And
    https://www.vegansociety.com/sites/default/files/uploads/Ripened%20by%20human%20determination.pdf
39 https://www.vegansociety.com/sites/default/files/uploads/Ripened%20by%20human%20determination.pdf
40 https://www.independent.co.uk/life-style/who-were-the-world-s-very-earliest-vegans-a7668831.html
41 https://www.theguardian.com/lifeandstyle/2021/oct/10/from-fringe-to-mainstream-how-millions-got-a-taste-for-going-vegan

42   https://www.vegansociety.com/about-us/history
43   https://wtvox.com/lifestyle/2019-the-world-of-vegan-but-how-many-vegans-are-in-the-world/
44   https://fridaysforfuture.org
45   https://www.bbc.com/future/article/20200122-are-there-health-benefits-to-going-vegan

02 MEAT CORRUPTION

1   https://www.goodreads.com/quotes/8144295-the-world-will-not-be-destroyed-by-those-who-do
2   https://www.idtechex.com/en/research-article/the-meat-industry-is-unsustainable/20231
3   https://ourworldindata.org/meat-production
4   https://www.nationalgeographic.com/culture/article/neolithic-agricultural-revolution
5   https://en.wikipedia.org/wiki/Organicism
6   https://www.ncbi.nlm.nih.gov/pmc/articles/PMC2946087/
7   U.S. Food and Drug Administration. Letter to The Honorable Louise M. Slaughter: Sales of Antibacterial Drugs in Kilograms. Washington D.C.; 2010. And http://www.foodsystemprimer.org/food-production/industrialization-of-agriculture/
8   http://www.foodsystemprimer.org/food-production/industrialization-of-agriculture/
9   https://jia.sipa.columbia.edu/removing-meat-subsidy-our-cognitive-dissonance-around-animal-agriculture#6
10   https://jia.sipa.columbia.edu/removing-meat-subsidy-our-cognitive-dissonance-around-animal-agriculture#6 and David Robinson Simon, Meatonomics. Berkeley, California. Conari Press, 2013.]
11   https://www.aei.org/carpe-diem/farm-subsidies-gone-wild-cows-in-europe-earn-more-per-day-2-20-than-1-2-billion-poor-people/]
12   https://www.surgeactivism.org/articles/uk-farming-subsidies-and-brexit-explained and https://www.surgeactivism.org/animalagsubsidiesexplained
13   https://text.npr.org/790261705 and https://www.surgeactivism.org/animalagsubsidiesexplained
14   https://hal.archives-ouvertes.fr/hal-02891112/document
15   https://ourworldindata.org/grapher/meat-supply-per-person?tab=table
16   Source for pricing: www.walmart.com
17   https://www.who.int/bulletin/archives/78(7)902.pdf
18   http://www.spiegel.de/wirtschaft/ruegenwalder-muehle-verkauft-vegetarische-wurst-a-1023898.html
19   https://www.slowfood.com/become-a-beefatarian-the-absurd-eu-campaign-calling-for-an-increase-in-meat-consumption/
20   https://ec.europa.eu/chafea/agri/en/campaigns/proud-eu-beef
21   https://ec.europa.eu/commission/presscorner/detail/en/IP_21_3541
22   https://www.foodnavigator.com/Article/2020/08/28/New-campaign-champions-environmental-benefits-of-meat and www.sustainablebritishmeat.org
23   https://www.farminguk.com/news/-eat-balanced-meat-and-dairy-ad-campaign-goes-live_57292.html
24   https://cancerres.aacrjournals.org/content/43/5/2150
25   https://www.dietaryguidelines.gov/sites/default/files/2020-12/Dietary_Guidelines_for_Americans_2020-2025.pdf
     https://health.gov/sites/default/files/2019-10/DietaryGuidelines2010.pdf
     https://health.gov/sites/default/files/2019-09/2015-2020_Dietary_Guidelines.pdf
     MyVeganPlate Image: https://www.vrg.org/nutshell/MyVeganPlate.pdf
     https://MyPlate.gov
26   https://www.nytimes.com/2020/05/21/opinion/coronavirus-meat-vegetarianism.html
27   https://culturedbeef.org/what-cultured-meat
28   https://www.reuters.com/article/us-food-tech-labmeat-idUSKCN1U41W8
29   https://www.idtechex.com/en/research-report/cultured-meat-2021-2041-technologies-markets-forecasts/815
30   https://www.idtechex.com/en/research-report/cultured-meat-2021-2041-technologies-markets-forecasts/815

03 REBEL WITH A CAUSE

1   https://www.megainteresting.com/arts-culture/article/albert-einsteins-most-famous-quotes-601576757467
2   https://en.wikipedia.org/wiki/Western_pattern_diet
3   https://www.who.int/news/item/15-07-2019-world-hunger-is-still-not-going-down-after-three-years-and-obesity-is-still-growing-un-report
4   https://www.brainpickings.org/2016/06/17/albert-camus-the-rebel/

04 LIVESTOCK

1   https://mainstreetvegan.net/veganism-and-martin-luther-king-jr-s-legacy-of-love-by-elisa-stone-mvlce/
2   The term cognitive dissonance describes the mental discomfort that comes from holding two conflicting beliefs, values, or attitudes. We naturally tend to seek consistency in our attitudes and perceptions, so this conflict often causes unease and discomfort.
3   "FAOSTAT". www.fao.org. Archived from the original on 11 May 2017. Retrieved 25 October 2019.
     And https://en.wikipedia.org/wiki/Animal_slaughter#cite_note-2
4   https://www.heromovement.net/blog/vegan-quotes/
5   https://en.wikipedia.org/wiki/Sentient_beings_(Buddhism)
6   https://en.wikipedia.org/wiki/Sentience
7   https://en.wikipedia.org/wiki/Ag-gag
8   https://www.theguardian.com/books/2015/sep/25/industrial-farming-one-worst-crimes-history-ethical-question
9   https://en.wikipedia.org/wiki/Ag-gag#cite_note-5
10   "Ag Gag: Safeguarding Industry Secrets by Punishing the Messenger" Archived 2014-07-18 at the Wayback Machine, Food Integrity Campaign, Retrieved June 25, 2013.
11   https://www.nrcs.usda.gov/wps/portal/nrcs/main/national/plantsanimals/livestock/afo/
12   https://en.wikipedia.org/wiki/Cattle
13   https://www.farmtransparency.org/kb/48-age-animals-slaughtered
14   https://www.peta.org/issues/animals-used-for-food/factory-farming/cows/cow-transport-slaughter/
15   https://www.nhes.org/animal-info-2/factory-farmed-animals-2/factory-farmed-cows/
16   https://www.peta.org/issues/animals-used-for-food/factory-farming/pigs/pig-transport-slaughter/
17   https://www.nhes.org/factory-farmed-pigs/
18   https://www.avma.org/sites/default/files/resources/swine_castration_bgnd.pdf
19   https://thehumaneleague.org/article/factory-farmed-pigs
20   https://www.wellbeingintlstudiesrepository.org/cgi/viewcontent.cgi?article=1042&context=acwp_asie
21   https://www.theguardian.com/books/2015/sep/25/industrial-farming-one-worst-crimes-history-ethical-question
22   https://www.weforum.org/agenda/2019/02/chart-of-the-day-this-is-how-many-animals-we-eat-each-year/
23   https://www.theguardian.com/environment/2016/apr/24/real-cost-of-roast-chicken-animal-welfare-farms
24   https://www.worldanimalprotection.org/news/10-facts-you-should-know-about-factory-farmed-chickens
25   https://www.britannica.com/explore/savingearth/the-difficult-lives-and-deaths-of-factory-farmed-chickens
26   https://www.theguardian.com/environment/2016/apr/24/real-cost-of-roast-chicken-animal-welfare-farms
27   https://thehumaneleague.org/article/factory-farmed-chickens
28   https://thehumaneleague.org/article/factory-farmed-chickens
29   https://www.latimes.com/archives/la-xpm-2003-nov-22-me-chipper22-story.html
30   https://www.peta.org/issues/animals-used-for-food/factory-farming/chickens/
31   https://www.peta.org/issues/animals-used-for-food/factory-farming/fish/aquafarming/
32   http://www.fishcount.org.uk/published/std/fishcountexecsummary.pdf
33   "FAOSTAT". www.fao.org. Archived from the original on May 11, 2017. Retrieved October 25, 2019. And https://en.wikipedia.org/wiki/Meat#cite_note-27
34   The Vegan Calculator: https://thevegancalculator.com/animal-slaughter/ And Bite Size Vegan: https://bitesizevegan.org/ethics/quantifying-suffering-cruelty-by-the-numbers/

05 ENVIRONMENT

1. https://www.theguardian.com/books/2019/sep/28/meat-of-the-matter-the-inconvenient-truth-about-what-we-eat
2. https://www.livekindly.co/inconvenient-sequel-overlooks-truth/
3. https://www.nrdc.org/stories/greenhouse-effect-101
4. https://www.theguardian.com/world/2021/jun/28/canada-hits-record-temperature-of-461c-amid-heatwave
5. https://www.theguardian.com/environment/2021/jul/30/greenland-ice-sheet-florida-water-climate-crisis
6. Journal: https://3209a1b2-3bad-4874-bf51-8fc2702ffa6c.filesusr.com/ugd/8654c5_7c6128c4df8741ad876709bc81afcfca.pdf page 156;
Article: https://plantbasednews.org/news/environment/animal-agriculture-responsible-for-87-of-greenhouse-gas-emissions/
7. https://www.sierraclub.org/michigan/why-are-cafos-bad#waste
8. https://www.sciencedirect.com/science/article/pii/S2212371713000024
9. https://ourworldindata.org/global-land-for-agriculture
10. https://journals.law.stanford.edu/stanford-environmental-law-journal-elj/blog/leading-cause-everything-one-industry-destroying-our-planet-and-our-ability-thrive-it
11. https://www.scientificamerican.com/article/earth-talks-daily-destruction/
12. www.savetheamazon.org/rainforeststats.htm
13. https://www.livekindly.co/inconvenient-sequel-overlooks-truth/
14. https://www.theworldcounts.com/challenges/planet-earth/forests-and-deserts/rate-of-deforestation/story
15. https://www.wri.org/insights/2021-must-be-turning-point-forests-2020-data-shows-us-why
16. https://www.theguardian.com/environment/2021/jul/14/amazon-rainforest-now-emitting-more-co2-than-it-absorbs
17. https://www.siwi.org/facts-and-statistics/6-food-agriculture-and-bioenergy/
18. https://unesdoc.unesco.org/ark:/48223/pf0000215492
and https://www.siwi.org/facts-and-statistics/6-food-agriculture-and-bioenergy/
19. https://waterfootprint.org/media/downloads/Report-48-WaterFootprint-AnimalProducts-Vol1_1.pdf and
https://waterfootprint.org/en/water-footprint/product-water-footprint/water-footprint-crop-and-animal-products/
20. http://www.unesco.org/new/fileadmin/MULTIMEDIA/FIELD/Venice/pdf/special_events/bozza_scheda_DOW04_1.0.pdf and https://www.statista.com/statistics/1092652/volume-of-water-to-produce-a-liter-of-milk-by-type/
21. https://www.ciwf.com/media/1230930/CIWF-Strategic-Plan-2013-2017.pdf
22. https://www.nrcs.usda.gov/wps/portal/nrcs/main/national/plantsanimals/livestock/afo/
23. https://www.sierraclub.org/michigan/why-are-cafos-bad#waste
24. https://www.theguardian.com/environment/2017/aug/01/meat-industry-dead-zone-gulf-of-mexico-environment-pollution
25. https://www.nationalgeographic.com/environment/article/dead-zones
26. https://en.wikipedia.org/wiki/Dead_zone_(ecology)#cite_note-:12-2
27. https://www.theguardian.com/books/2015/sep/25/industrial-farming-one-worst-crimes-history-ethical-question
28. https://www.ipbes.net/news/Media-Release-Global-Assessment
29. https://www.ipbes.net/news/Media-Release-Global-Assessment
30. https://www.bbc.com/news/world-latin-america-41107862
31. https://en.wikipedia.org/wiki/Western_pattern_diet
32. https://en.wikipedia.org/wiki/Western_pattern_diet
33. https://www.sciencedirect.com/science/article/pii/S0048969720328709#f0005
34. https://www.nationalgeographic.com/foodfeatures/evolution-of-diet/

06 HEALTH

1 https://www.sciencedirect.com/science/article/pii/S0014299918303595
2 Taylor LH, Latham SM, Woolhouse ME (2001). "Risk factors for human disease emergence". Philosophical Transactions of the Royal Society B: Biological Sciences. 356 (1411): 983–89. doi:10.1098/rstb.2001.0888. PMC 1088493. PMID 11516376.
3 Taylor LH, Latham SM, Woolhouse ME (2001). "Risk factors for human disease emergence". Philosophical Transactions of the Royal Society B: Biological Sciences. 356 (1411): 983–89. doi:10.1098/rstb.2001.0888. PMC 1088493. PMID 11516376.
4 https://www.theguardian.com/environment/2020/apr/08/human-impact-on-wildlife-to-blame-for-spread-of-viruses-says-study-aoe
5 https://en.wikipedia.org/wiki/Natural_reservoir
6 https://environmentlive.unep.org/media/docs/assessments/UNEP_Frontiers_2016_report_emerging_issues_of_environmental_concern.pdf
7 https://www.theguardian.com/world/2020/mar/28/is-factory-farming-to-blame-for-coronavirus
8 https://pubmed.ncbi.nlm.nih.gov/24531761/
9 https://www.ncbi.nlm.nih.gov/pmc/articles/PMC2720273/ and https://www.theguardian.com/commentisfree/2020/apr/16/coronavirus-covid-19-pandemic-food-animals
10 https://en.wikipedia.org/wiki/Bovine_spongiform_encephalopathy
11 https://www.nationalgeographic.co.uk/science-and-technology/2020/04/experts-warned-of-pandemic-decades-ago-why-werent-we-ready
12 https://www.ncbi.nlm.nih.gov/pmc/articles/PMC1963309/
13 https://www.theguardian.com/commentisfree/2020/apr/16/coronavirus-covid-19-pandemic-food-animals
14 https://www.worldometers.info/coronavirus/coronavirus-death-toll/
15 https://www.cidrap.umn.edu/news-perspective/2003/05/estimates-sars-death-rates-revised-upward
16 https://www.who.int/health-topics/middle-east-respiratory-syndrome-coronavirus-mers#tab=tab_1
17 https://www.who.int/news-room/fact-sheets/detail/ebola-virus-disease
18 https://www.theguardian.com/world/2020/mar/28/is-factory-farming-to-blame-for-coronavirus
19 https://www.worldometers.info/coronavirus/coronavirus-death-rate/
20 http://apps.who.int/iris/bitstream/handle/10665/112642/9789241564748_eng.pdf
21 https://www.fda.gov/animal-veterinary/antimicrobial-resistance/timeline-fda-action-antimicrobial-resistance
22 https://www.pewtrusts.org/en/research-and-analysis/articles/2020/01/16/antibiotic-sales-for-animal-agriculture-increase-again-after-a-two-year-decline
23 https://www.theworldcounts.com/challenges/consumption/foods-and-beverages/antibiotics-used-for-livestock/story
24 https://www.who.int/news/item/07-11-2017-stop-using-antibiotics-in-healthy-animals-to-prevent-the-spread-of-antibiotic-resistance
25 https://www.peta.org/issues/animals-used-for-food/factory-farming/cows/beef-industry/
26 https://www.cdc.gov/drugresistance/biggest-threats.html
27 https://www.who.int/news/item/07-11-2017-stop-using-antibiotics-in-healthy-animals-to-prevent-the-spread-of-antibiotic-resistance
28 https://www.who.int/mediacentre/news/statements/2011/whd_20110407/en/
29 https://en.wikipedia.org/wiki/Zoonosis
30 https://en.wikipedia.org/wiki/Zoonosis#/media/File:Figure_3-_Examples_of_Zoonotic_Diseases_and_Their_Affected_Populations_(6323431516).jpg
31 https://www.foodandwine.com/cooking-techniques/albert-einstein-genius-birthday-boy-vegetarian-vegan
32 https://en.wikipedia.org/wiki/Western_pattern_diet
33 https://www.ncbi.nlm.nih.gov/books/NBK493173/
34 https://en.wikipedia.org/wiki/Western_pattern_diet
35 https://pubmed.ncbi.nlm.nih.gov/30928934/
36 http://www.milkfacts.info/Milk%20Microbiology/Microbial%20Standards.htm
37 https://en.wikipedia.org/wiki/Western_pattern_diet
38 https://vegnews.com/2021/6/breast-cancer-study-meat-dairy
39 https://en.wikipedia.org/wiki/Western_pattern_diet
40 https://economictimes.indiatimes.com/magazines/panache/sugar-is-a-greater-danger-than-gunpowder-says-sapiens-author-yuval-noah-harari/articleshow/63574089.cms
41 https://www.who.int/news-room/fact-sheets/detail/obesity-and-overweight
42 https://www.ncbi.nlm.nih.gov/pmc/articles/PMC7721435/
43 https://www.ncbi.nlm.nih.gov/pmc/articles/PMC5507106/

44   https://www.nature.com/articles/s41591-020-01209-1
45   https://idf.org/aboutdiabetes/what-is-diabetes/facts-figures.html
46   https://www.who.int/news-room/fact-sheets/detail/diabetes
47   https://www.who.int/news-room/fact-sheets/detail/diabetes
48   https://www.ncbi.nlm.nih.gov/pmc/articles/PMC3173026/
49   https://www.sciencedaily.com/releases/2017/09/170905134506.htm
50   https://www.ncbi.nlm.nih.gov/pmc/articles/PMC2677007/
51   https://nutritionstudies.org/my-type-2-diabetic-patients-transformed-their-health-through-diet/
52   https://www.nih.gov/news-events/nih-research-matters/eating-red-meat-daily-triples-heart-disease-related-chemical
53   https://en.wikipedia.org/wiki/Western_pattern_diet
54   https://jamanetwork.com/journals/jama/fullarticle/2728487
55   https://www.ucsfhealth.org/education/cholesterol-content-of-foods
56   https://www.cdc.gov/heartdisease/facts.htm
57   https://www.pcrm.org/good-nutrition/nutrition-information/lowering-cholesterol-with-a-plant-based-diet AND Yokoyama Y, Levin SM, Barnard ND. Association between plant-based diets and plasma lipids: a systematic review and meta-analysis. Nutr Rev. Published online August 21, 2017.
58   https://www.ahajournals.org/doi/10.1161/JAHA.119.012865
59   https://acsjournals.onlinelibrary.wiley.com/doi/10.3322/caac.21660
60   https://www.who.int/news-room/q-a-detail/cancer-carcinogenicity-of-the-consumption-of-red-meat-and-processed-meat
61   https://www.who.int/news-room/q-a-detail/cancer-carcinogenicity-of-the-consumption-of-red-meat-and-processed-meat and https://publications.iarc.fr/Book-And-Report-Series/Iarc-Monographs-On-The-Identification-Of-Carcinogenic-Hazards-To-Humans/Red-Meat-And-Processed-Meat-2018
62   https://cancerdiscovery.aacrjournals.org/content/early/2021/06/11/2159-8290.CD-20-1656 and https://medicalxpress.com/news/2021-06-biological-links-red-meat-colorectal.html
63   https://www.pnas.org/content/116/32/16036 and https://health.ucsd.edu/news/releases/Pages/2019-07-22-evolutionary-gene-loss-may-help-explain-human-heart-attacks.aspx
64   https://vegnews.com/2021/6/breast-cancer-study-meat-dairy and https://pubmed.ncbi.nlm.nih.gov/33962395/
65   https://www.tandfonline.com/doi/abs/10.1080/10408398.2016.1138447?journalCode=bfsn20
66   https://jumdjournal.net/article/view/2892
67   https://www.ted.com/talks/samuel_cohen_alzheimer_s_is_not_normal_aging_and_we_can_cure_it/transcript
68   https://www.ncbi.nlm.nih.gov/pmc/articles/PMC6846186/
69   https://www.bluezones.com/2019/10/the-2-foods-that-combat-alzheimers-disease-other-lifestyle-factors-to-reduce-your-risk-of-cognitive-decline/#
70   https://www.bluezones.com/2018/11/a-greek-islands-ancient-secret-to-avoiding-alzheimers/#
71   https://www.cochranelibrary.com/cdsr/doi/10.1002/14651858.CD003177.pub3/full
72   https://pubmed.ncbi.nlm.nih.gov/29355094/
73   https://www.ahajournals.org/doi/10.1161/01.ATV.0000038493.65177.94
74   https://plantbasednews.org/your-health/faqs-and-mythbusting/fish-not-health-food-why/
75   https://epi.grants.cancer.gov/diet/foodsources/top-food-sources-report-02212020.pdf
76   https://epi.grants.cancer.gov/diet/foodsources/top-food-sources-report-02212020.pdf
77   https://academic.oup.com/ije/article-abstract/49/5/1526/5743492
78   https://www.eurekalert.org/pub_releases/2019-10/aoa-mcr101819.php
79   https://www.theguardian.com/lifeandstyle/2003/dec/13/foodanddrink.weekend
80   https://academic.oup.com/ije/article-abstract/49/5/1526/5743492
81   https://www.ncbi.nlm.nih.gov/pmc/articles/PMC6683061/
82   https://www.theguardian.com/lifeandstyle/2003/dec/13/foodanddrink.weekend
83   https://www.hsph.harvard.edu/nutritionsource/calcium/
84   https://en.wikipedia.org/wiki/Western_pattern_diet
85   https://www.nytimes.com/2012/10/28/magazine/the-island-where-people-forget-to-die.html
86   https://www.nationalgeographic.com/magazine/article/these-traditional-diets-from-the-blue-zones-can-lead-to-long-lives-feature
87   https://www.nationalgeographic.com/magazine/article/these-traditional-diets-from-the-blue-zones-can-lead-to-long-lives-feature
88   https://en.wikipedia.org/wiki/Western_pattern_diet
89   https://www.google.com/search?client=firefox-b-d&q=how+many+people+have+died+from+covid as at 5th July 2021)
90   https://www.who.int/news-room/fact-sheets/detail/noncommunicable-diseases
91   https://www.telegraph.co.uk/science/2018/04/26/third-early-deaths-could-prevented-everyone-giving-meat-harvard/

07 SOCIAL STUDIES

1   https://www.ciwf.org.uk/media/7425974/industrial-livestock-production-the-twin-myths-of-efficiency-and-necessity.pdf
2   https://news.cornell.edu/stories/1997/08/us-could-feed-800-million-people-grain-livestock-eat
3   https://www.theguardian.com/news/2019/jan/28/can-we-ditch-intensive-farming-and-still-feed-the-world
4   https://www.aljazeera.com/economy/2021/5/25/bbin-2020-more-people-displaced-by-extreme-climate-than-conflict
5   https://news.un.org/en/story/2021/03/1087702
6   https://www.meatpoultry.com/articles/14493-study-quantifies-the-economic-impact-of-meat-industry
7   https://www.meatinstitute.org/index.php?ht=d/sp/i/47465/pid/47465
8   https://www.hrw.org/report/2010/12/11/rights-line/human-rights-watch-work-abuses-against-migrants-2010
9   https://mercyforanimals.org/blog/dairy-farm-worker-drowns/
10   https://foodispower.org/human-labor-slavery/factory-farm-workers/
11   "Concentrated Animal Feedlot Operations (CAFOs) Chemicals Associated with Air Emissions." Prepared by the CAFO subcommittee of the Michigan Department of Environmental Quality (MDEQ) Toxics Steering Group (TSG). 2006. http://www.michigan.gov/documents/CAFOs-Chemicals_Associated_with_Air_Emissions_5-10-06_158862_7.pdf (5/27/10) and https://foodispower.org/human-labor-slavery/factory-farm-workers/
12   Concentrated Animal Feedlot Operations (CAFOs) Chemicals Associated with Air Emissions." Prepared by the CAFO subcommittee of the Michigan Department of Environmental Quality (MDEQ) Toxics Steering Group (TSG). 2006. http://www.michigan.gov/documents/CAFOs-Chemicals_Associated_with_Air_Emissions_5-10-06_158862_7.pdf (5/27/10)
13   https://vegnews.com/2013/4/inside-the-life-of-a-factory-farm-worker
14   https://www.oxfamamerica.org/livesontheline/
15   https://vegnews.com/2013/4/inside-the-life-of-a-factory-farm-worker
16   Lewis, Cora (18 February 2018). "America's Largest Meat Producer Averages One Amputation Per Month". Buzzfeed News. Retrieved 23 May 2019. And https://en.wikipedia.org/wiki/Slaughterhouse
17   https://en.wikipedia.org/wiki/Slaughterhouse and Eisnitz, Gail A. Slaughterhouse. Prometheus Books, 1997, cited in Torres, Bob. Making a Killing. AK Press, 2007, p. 46.
18   https://www.theguardian.com/environment/2019/sep/18/us-moves-to-scrap-speed-limits-on-pig-slaughter-lines and https://abcnews.go.com/Health/wireStory/pork-group-asks-usda-support-faster-slaughterhouse-speeds-77897261
19   Baran, B. E.; Rogelberg, S. G.; Clausen, T (2016). "Routinized killing of animals: Going beyond dirty work and prestige to understand the well-being of slaughterhouse workers". Organization. 23 (3): 351–69. doi:10.1177/1350508416629456. S2CID 148368906. And https://en.wikipedia.org/wiki/Slaughterhouse
20   Fitzgerald, A. J.; Kalof, L. (2009). "Slaughterhouses and Increased Crime Rates: An Empirical Analysis of the Spillover From "The Jungle" Into the Surrounding Community". Organization & Environment. 22 (2): 158–84. doi:10.1177/1350508416629456. S2CID 148368906. And https://en.wikipedia.org/wiki/Slaughterhouse
21   https://www.peta.org/issues/animal-companion-issues/animal-companion-factsheets/animal-abuse-human-abuse-partners-crime/
22   Nadimpalli, Maya. "Persistence of livestock-associated antibiotic-resistant Staphylococcus aureus among industrial hog operation workers in North Carolina over 14 days." Occupational & Environmental Medicine, 72(2) (September 8, 2014). Retrieved May 31, 2018, from https://oem.bmj.com/content/early/2014/09/05/oemed-2014-102095.info and https://foodprint.org/issues/what-happens-to-animal-waste/
23   https://foodprint.org/issues/what-happens-to-animal-waste/ and US Environmental Protection Agency. "Basic Information about Nonpoint Source (NPS) Pollution. EPA, (n.d.). Retrieved May 31, 2018 from https://www.epa.gov/nps/basic-information-about-nonpoint-source-nps-pollution
24   https://www.doh.wa.gov/Portals/1/Documents/Pubs/331-214.pdf
25   http://animalstudies.msu.edu/Slaughterhouses_and_Increased_Crime_Rates.pdf and https://www.huffpost.com/entry/plight-of-factory-farm-workers_b_5662261
26   Carol J. Hodne, Concentrating on Clean Water: The Challenge of Concentrated Animal Feeding Operations, IA Policy Project (Apr. 2005), at 28, available at http://www.iowapolicyproject.org/2005docs/050406-cafo-fullx.pdf . And https://www.animallaw.info/article/detailed-discussion-concentrated-animal-feeding-operations
27   https://www.theguardian.com/us-news/2020/apr/28/trump-executive-order-meat-processing-plants-coronavirus

28 https://www.dol.gov/newsroom/releases/osha/osha20200428-1
29 https://www.theguardian.com/world/2020/may/02/meat-plant-workers-us-coronavirus-war
30 https://www.theguardian.com/world/2020/may/02/meat-plant-workers-us-coronavirus-war
31 Reported at the July 24-26 meeting of the Canadian Society of Animal Science, Montreal.
32 https://www.idtechex.com/en/research-article/the-meat-industry-is-unsustainable/20231
33 https://en.wikipedia.org/wiki/Western_pattern_diet

08 LIFE ON THE SPECTRUM
1   https://www.independent.co.uk/life-style/food-and-drink/carnism-why-love-dogs-eat-pigs-wear-cows-leather-pork-dr-melanie-joy-vegan-psychology-a7932621.html
2   https://www.peta.org/about-peta/faq/what-is-speciesism/
3   https://en.wikipedia.org/wiki/Carnism
4   https://www.pure.ed.ac.uk/ws/files/24434085/Piazza_etal_A_2015_Rationalizing_Meat_Consumption_The_4Ns.pdf
5   https://www.pure.ed.ac.uk/ws/files/24434085/Piazza_etal_A_2015_Rationalizing_Meat_Consumption_The_4Ns.pdf
6   https://www.slowfood.com/press-release/slow-food-launches-the-worldwide-campaign-meat-the-change-to-change-peoples-meat-eating-habits/
7   https://en.wikipedia.org/wiki/Western_pattern_diet

09 REBEL VEGAN STARTER KIT
1   https://www.wfp.org/zero-hunger
2   https://www.forbes.com/sites/jeffmcmahon/2019/04/04/meat-and-agriculture-are-worse-for-the-climate-than-dirty-energy-steven-chu-says/
3   https://news.cornell.edu/stories/1997/08/us-could-feed-800-million-people-grain-livestock-eat
4   http://shrinkthatfootprint.com/food-carbon-footprint-diet and https://www.cowspiracy.com/facts
5   Robbins, John. Diet for a New America, StillPoint Publishing, 1987, p. 352 and https://www.cowspiracy.com/facts
6   Oppenlander, Richard A. Food Choice and Sustainability: Why Buying Local, Eating Less Meat, and Taking Baby Steps Won't Work. Minneapolis, MN : Langdon Street, 2013. Print. And https://www.cowspiracy.com/facts
7   https://en.wikipedia.org/wiki/Western_pattern_diet
8   http://www.ncbi.nlm.nih.gov/pubmed/24717365 and https://nutritionfacts.org/video/do-flexitarians-live-longer/
9   https://en.wikipedia.org/wiki/Western_pattern_diet
10 http://www.ncbi.nlm.nih.gov/pubmed/21411506 and https://nutritionfacts.org/video/do-flexitarians-live-longer/
11 https://en.wikipedia.org/wiki/Western_pattern_diet
12 http://www.ncbi.nlm.nih.gov/pubmed/24524383 and https://nutritionfacts.org/video/do-flexitarians-live-longer/
13 https://www.cowspiracy.com/facts

10 THE HOW
1   https://faunalytics.org/wp-content/uploads/2015/06/Faunalytics_Current-Former-Vegetarians_Full-Report.pdf
2   https://juniperpublishers.com/ctoij/CTOIJ.MS.ID.555906.php and https://jumdjournal.net/article/view/2892
3   https://v-dog.com/blogs/v-dog-blog/bramble-the-collies-secrets-to-living-to-age-25
4   https://www.ncbi.nlm.nih.gov/books/NBK80015/
5   https://pubmed.ncbi.nlm.nih.gov/19211820/
6   https://www.pcrm.org/good-nutrition/nutrition-information/soy-and-health
7   https://www.vegansociety.com/go-vegan/why-go-vegan/honey-industry
8   https://vegan.com/info/answers/#honey
9   https://www.vegansociety.com/go-vegan/why-go-vegan/honey-industry

11 EMPOWERMENT

1   https://veganorigo.com/en/pages/famous-vegans/
2   https://metro.co.uk/2019/04/13/man-who-ate-raw-pigs-head-at-vegan-festival-stabbed-four-classmates-at-school-9184229/
3   https://london.eater.com/2019/7/23/20707059/squirrel-eating-pro-meat-anti-vegan-protest-soho-alt-right-youtube-channel
4   https://journals.sagepub.com/doi/abs/10.1177/1368430215618253 and https://www.theguardian.com/lifeandstyle/2019/oct/25/why-do-people-hate-vegans
5   https://www.peta.org/living/food/really-natural-truth-humans-eating-meat/
6   https://www.smithsonianmag.com/science-nature/where-do-humans-really-rank-on-the-food-chain-180948053/
7   Rizzo NS, Jaceldo-Siegl K, Sabate J, Fraser GE. Nutrient profiles of vegetarian and nonvegetarian dietary patterns. J Acad Nutr Diet. 2013 Dec;113(12):1610-9. And https://gamechangersmovie.com/protein/
8   USDA Food Composition Databases and https://gamechangersmovie.com/food/protein/
9   https://switch4good.org/how-dairy-affects-childrens-health/
10 https://www.medicalnewstoday.com/articles/325425#nutritional-values
11 https://www.pnas.org/content/117/24/13596
12 https://www.independent.co.uk/news/world/asia/yulin-dog-meat-festival-explainer-what-it-when-start-banned-controversy-a8410426.html
13 https://en.wikipedia.org/wiki/Whaling_in_the_Faroe_Islands
14 https://www.humanesociety.org/resources/cage-free-vs-battery-cage-eggs
15 https://www.theguardian.com/lifeandstyle/shortcuts/2017/feb/28/what-does-free-range-actually-mean-its-complicated
16 https://en.wikipedia.org/wiki/Western_pattern_diet
17 https://www.bda.uk.com/resource/british-dietetic-association-confirms-well-planned-vegan-diets-can-support-healthy-living-in-people-of-all-ages.html
18 https://pubmed.ncbi.nlm.nih.gov/19562864/
19 https://pubmed.ncbi.nlm.nih.gov/12778049/
20 https://ods.od.nih.gov/factsheets/VitaminB12-HealthProfessional/
21 https://ods.od.nih.gov/factsheets/VitaminB12-HealthProfessional/

14 APPENDICES

1   https://www.statista.com/statistics/183785/per-capita-consumption-of-cheese-in-the-us-since-2000/ and https://www.ncbi.nlm.nih.gov/books/NBK45515/ (figure 4.4)
2   https://www.who.int/news/item/07-11-2017-stop-using-antibiotics-in-healthy-animals-to-prevent-the-spread-of-antibiotic-resistance
1   https://www.sciencedirect.com/science/article/pii/S1198743X15010307
2   https://www.who.int/news-room/fact-sheets/detail/campylobacter
3   https://www.theguardian.com/world/2014/jul/23/-sp-revealed-dirty-secret-uk-poultry-industry-chicken-campylobacter
4   https://www.cdc.gov/campylobacter/index.html
5   https://www.theguardian.com/world/2014/jul/23/-sp-revealed-dirty-secret-uk-poultry-industry-chicken-campylobacter
6   https://en.wikipedia.org/wiki/Staphylococcus_aureus and https://www.intechopen.com/chapters/66903
7   https://en.wikipedia.org/wiki/Staphylococcus_aureus
8   www.sciencedaily.com/releases/2011/04/110415083153.htm
9   https://www.cdc.gov/drugresistance/biggest-threats.html
10 https://www.who.int/news-room/fact-sheets/detail/e-coli
11 https://www.ecdc.europa.eu/en/escherichia-coli-ecoli

Made in the USA
Middletown, DE
30 November 2021